From Islam
to Christianity

From Islam to Christianity

A True Story of Faith and Persecution

"A very important and powerful
book that should be read by everyone
who cares about persecution of
Christians and religious freedom."

Isah Jesse Abraham

XULON PRESS ELITE

Xulon Press
2301 Lucien Way #415
Maitland, FL 32751
407.339.4217
www.xulonpress.com

WARNING
The following content contains graphic and disturbing imagery. Viewer discretion is advised.

Paperback ISBN-13: 978-1-6628-2183-7
Ebook ISBN-13: 978-1-6628-2184-4

Contents

Foreword. vii

Introduction and Acknowledgments xi

1. Born Into It. 1

2. My Parents' Love for Me 5

3. After My Encounter With Jesus 19

4. I Now Know the Truth. 29

5. I Am Convicted to Be a Christian 47

6. I Am Born Again. 79

7. The Divinity and the Humanity of
    Jesus Christ. 91

8. Birth, Crucifixion, Death, Burial,
    Resurrection, and Ascension of Jesus 99

9. The Persecution Begins 139

About the Author 157

Foreword

It was in March 2018, as we shared ministry at a Pastors Training Conference in their home country of Nigeria, that I first met Pastor Isah Jesse Abraham and his wife Damaris Zainab Isah. Little did I realize then the amazing story of danger, suffering, and great loss they have experienced since leaving Islam in 1995. The Abrahams' decision to follow Christ has resulted in many fruitful years of service to Him as pastors, church planters, and evangelists throughout Nigeria. However, as you will learn in the pages ahead, it has not come without personal cost and danger.

Pastor Isah is a former Muslim Imam. The Arabic word Imam means a leader or model, in a general sense. An Imam leads Muslim worshippers in prayer. As a young man, as a *Ladan* at the mosque, he was the pride and joy of his devout Muslim family as his voice rang out over their Nigerian village with daily calls to prayer and the weekly call to public worship.

But when he decided to follow Jesus Christ, a raging hatred from some of his closest family and friends fell upon Pastor Isah, his wife, and his children. As a result, he came to know firsthand what our Lord meant when He said, *"Anyone who loves his father or mother more than Me is not worthy of Me; anyone who loves his son or daughter more than Me is not worthy of Me; and anyone who does not take up his cross and follow Me is not worthy of Me. Whoever finds his life will lose it, and whoever loses his life for My sake will find it."*

The pain and difficulties have not ceased, even twenty-five years later. With growing danger and threats of death against them, Jesse and Damaris Abraham were forced to seek religious asylum here in the United States. They had to leave their five children — four of whom are still minors — with relatives in Nigeria as they prayerfully await the U.S. State Department's approval for permanent religious asylum. Please pray that decision in their favor will come as soon as possible.

This book will serve as a great help in understanding some of the false teachings of Islam.

Pastor Jesse Abraham, a student and scholar of both the Quran and the true Bible, uncovers the *"doctrines of demons"* (1 Timothy 4:1) with the *"light of the knowledge of the glory of God in the face of Jesus Christ"* (2 Corinthians 4:6). This book may be a useful tool in the hands of the Holy Spirit to bring many hungry-hearted Muslims to faith in the Lord and provide information and insight to every Christian who desires to know more about the fastest-growing religion in the world.

Donald G. Kroah, D.Min.
Senior Pastor, Plymouth Haven Baptist Church, Alexandria, Virginia
Host of The Don Kroah Show, WAVA Radio, Washington, D.C.
President, Reach Africa Now, Inc.

Introduction and
Acknowledgments

P lease read this introduction carefully. It is essential that every reader understands why I wrote this book and understand my approach to this important subject.

Above all, it is vital that you understand that I do not hold any ill will toward those of my former religion, including my relatives, who have persecuted me and my fellow Christians. I forgive them for all that they have done, and fervently I pray not for their destruction, but that they may find the peace in Jesus Christ that I have found.

In this relatively brief book, I use all the knowledge that I have gained in both my Muslim education and my Christian education to guide everyone to the right path in life. I use my knowledge of the Quran to show how Jesus Christ is the greatest prophet in the Quran, and I use my knowledge of the Bible to prove that Jesus Christ is the Son of God, part of the triune God, and the creator of all things.

I pray for the Muslims in my extended family, among my former coworkers, among my childhood friends, and among the police and judicial authorities in Nigeria. I pray wholeheartedly that the God of the Bible — the Father, Son, and Holy Spirit — will lead them to the same belief that I have.

When Muslims that I have known urged me to choose Islam over Jesus, they did not know what they asked, because although I did choose Jesus, more importantly, He chose me! He came to me in a dream, just as He appeared in my wife's dreams, and showed me how to have everlasting life. He chose me, praise God, and showed me the truth of the Bible. How then could I have returned to Islam and rejected His adoption of me as a child in God's Kingdom?

I pray that He will also choose my family members, my friends, the members of the mosque I attended, and every Muslim who opposed me and my faith. I pray that God will choose them just as He chose me. I pray that God will open their minds and their hearts so that they may share in the love of Jesus Christ and the Kingdom of God.

Acknowledgments

In my journey of life and destiny, I have become aware of the truth that no one can stand alone as an island. Every great accomplishment is a result of so many contributions and input from many individuals who directly or indirectly affected my life with their gifts, knowledge, and wisdom.

The writing of this book would not have been possible were it not for the intellectual and spiritual giants of faith upon whose shoulders I stand, and the encouragement I received from them all. God Almighty, who called me out of the kingdom of darkness and planted my feet in the Kingdom of His marvelous light, brought these people into my life to provide me strength, even in the face of horrendous persecution.

To all of them, I want to express my profound appreciation. Many special people gave me much encouragement, but I can mention only a few by name. Dr. Donald G. Kroah, D.Min., Senior Pastor of Plymouth Haven Baptist Church in Alexandria, Virginia, host of the Don Kroah Show on WAVA Radio in Washington, D.C., and president of Reach Africa Now Inc., under the auspices of his church and ministry sponsored me and my family in the process of seeking religious asylum in the United States of America. Pastor Kroah also read the draft of this manuscript, gave valuable advice along the way, and wrote a foreword for this book. Pastor Kroah, you have supported me and my family in very many ways. I want to say with a deep sense of humility, thank you.

I also want to express my appreciation to Dr. and Dr. Mrs. Michael Gbenga Omotoso of the Chrysolite Fellowship Center, Baltimore, Maryland, for the enthusiasm, support, and stimulation they have accorded me as I wrote this book. Words cannot be enough.

I must also thank Dr. Derek Grier, Bishop of Grace Church in Dumfries, Virginia, for his contributions in offering advice on the manuscript of this book. His love and generosity are amazing. Words are not enough, but I say thank you again and again. Knowing Dr. Grier has been a huge blessing to me and my wife and an encouragement to us to always "think big."

I especially appreciate the patience and support of my editor, Clayton W. Boyce. I am thankful for his excitement about my book, for his painstaking editing and proofreading of the manuscript, and for being my publishing representative.

Most importantly, my deepest appreciation goes to my wife Damaris Zainab Isah, who has been equally supportive and understanding during the time of our intense persecutions. She stood through thick and thin, and she is still standing.

To my five children who have not given up on me as a father: You all have been there for me and with me in the face of adversities and impending dangers. I love you all and I say to you God is faithful, my dear children! You are not here with me, but I am always praying to God for your safety, and I am always praying that we will soon be reunited as one family again.

My thanks to God the Father, God the Son, and God the Holy Spirit, the author of eternal Salvation, who reached out for me and saved me from the religion of Islam, ushered me into Christianity, and made me a worthy laborer and vessel in His Kingdom.

Pastor Isah Jesse Abraham

Chapter One

Born Into It

I was born into a strong, devoted, Muslim family. My parents are descendants of Hausa Fulani from northern Nigeria, in West Africa. All my family members are still practicing Muslims. I am one of eleven children born into a noble family of Muslims. As I look back, I marvel that I left Islam and became a Christian pastor.

Because of my parents' Islamic faith, I was born into and grew up practicing Islam. Islam shaped every facet of my young life. Practicing Islam means that I accepted the five pillars of Islam, a must for all Muslims. I grew up as a Muslim to be aware of the teaching that says there is no God but Allah, and Muhammad is his messenger. That is what we were taught to believe in the Arabic school called Islamiyah.

From the time I began to comprehend things, I realized I was in an Arabic school learning how to read and write verses from the Quran in an Arabic language. Reciting the Quran, observing the five daily prayers, and fasting during the month of Ramadan were required when I was part of a Muslim family. Both at home and at school I was told to believe in the five pillars of Islam so that I would enter Paradise (Al-Jannah) when I die.

I was taught to believe there is no God but Allah, and Muhammad is his messenger. I had to pray five times a day, pay a tithe (Zakat) of my income to Allah, fast during the month of Ramadan, and attend a pilgrimage (Hajj).

In elementary school and post-elementary school, attending Arabic school was a must. When secular school classes ended, I attended afternoon classes at the Arabic school every day of the week except Thursday and Friday. It was a daily routine and to avoid it was to bring shame and disgrace to my Muslim family and ultimately was a sin of disobedience of Allah and his messenger.

In my teenage years I learned to obey Allah and his messenger in all they asked me to do as a Muslim. I had to follow the teachings of Muhammad until the end of my existence on earth. I was taught not to befriend any non-Muslim or associate myself with them because Allah and his messenger branded all non-Muslims as unbelievers and infidels. I was taught to have nothing to do with them, unless it was to convert them to the religion of Islam. I had to obey this because that is the teaching of Islam.

I was taught to prepare myself at all times to fight for the cause of Allah and his messenger. To fight for the cause of Allah in Islam means that I would fight and kill non-Muslims, those who are not followers of Allah and his messenger. This act is known as Jihad in Islam. Although I never in my life as a Muslim fought or killed non-Muslims, or refused to have them as my friends, I grew up with the consciousness of what the religion taught me.

Deeper in Islam

For more than twenty-seven years of my life, I learned and read the Quran, and I was a practicing Muslim. I rose up as a teenager to become a Ladan — someone who calls people to congregational prayer in the mosque. For so many years, as a young boy, I found myself going deeper and deeper into the Islamic religion I was born into.

Five times or more daily, I recited verses from chapter 1 of the Quran: *"In the name of Allah, the beneficent, the merciful. Praise be to Allah, lord of the worlds, the beneficent, the merciful. Master of the day of judgment, thee (alone) we worship; thee (alone) we ask for help. Show us the straight path, the path of those whom Thou hast favored; Not the (path) of those who earn thine anger nor of those who go astray.*" The underlined phrases above are of note because I will refer to them to stress a point in chapter six and in various places in this book.

I had to recite, *"In the name of Allah, the beneficent, the merciful,"* before I could do anything as a Muslim, whether it was to recite a verse or a chapter of the Quran or to start a prayer. I had to first recite those words if I was to be accepted by Allah. I had to show recognition of him as a deity in everything I did. That is the teaching of the religion of Islam that must be followed and that is what I was to practice until the day Jesus Christ came into my life.

Chapter Two

My Parents' Love for Me

My parents loved me in wonderful ways. They sent me to school to get an education. My father got me a job in a bank after I graduated from school. My parents found a wife for me when I was a teenager. My parents went out of their way to give me everything I wanted. Especially my father — he was there for me all the time. His reason for marrying for me at a tender age was because I had proven to be a responsible child who had grown so mature as to call the congregation to prayer in the mosque.

In fact, everybody in the community where I grew up was much impressed with the way I composed myself. I was well-behaved. My parents and my work colleagues were impressed with the way I used to call the congregational prayer. I did it as if

I had been born in an Arab country and had been an Arab all my life.

My Social Life

Growing up was so wonderful and interesting for me. Everything was going my way. I had a good job. I had married and had a child. I owned two cars. I had built a three-bedroom bungalow. I had money to spend. I had friends around me to cheer me up whenever we were out doing our teenage things. I socialized as I was growing up, but that did not temper my religious activities at all. I was able to set boundaries between what I did with friends and what I did as my religious activities. I did not drink beer, nor any strong drink, and I did not smoke, but some of my friends did all that stuff.

We partied and went to clubs together, but I was never a Casanova in their midst. I had the money to organize parties and buy beer and tobacco for them, but I did not drink or smoke. And after the partying, the next day I was back in the mosque calling people to prayer. What a life! Religion on one hand, and my social life on the other, and I did not see anything wrong with that at all. I thought that if I did not drink or smoke, I could party with friends and other women, even though I had a wife and child back at home. I did not see anything wrong with what I was doing because I was mandated by my Muslim religion to marry up to four wives.

How It All Began

Little did I know that my upbringing as a Muslim and my social life were preparations for me to be used by God. One day, I returned from work and I decided to go out in the evening to a club where I could relax. I invited one of my friends to go in my car. The club was my usual place of relaxation. We went into the club and sat down, and we ordered chapman drinks and steaks. A chapman drink is a Nigerian cocktail usually made of grenadine syrup, black currant, orange soda, and lemon-lime soda. It may have alcohol or not. I drank mine without alcohol.

While we were eating and drinking, I saw a young lady and her friend sit down near us. I asked my friend to call her over. Her name was Damaris Satmak Dakwal. She was a young lady who had just finished school and had come to visit her friend in Kaduna State Nigeria. Her friend had taken her to the club where we met. I introduced myself and we had a little conversation until we all departed.

The next evening, we were back at the same club and there was that same young lady again.

We talked again and she realized I was the same guy she had met the previous night. She sat with us and we went home together. She was nice to me and we began dating regularly. At the time, I had no idea Jesus Christ would use this lady for my salvation.

Am I in Love?

Remember that I was a young man with a wife and child. I was already building a family. I was a Muslim young man who impressed so many people with my upbringing and the way I did things. And here I am with a lady that I had just met and had started going out with just a few days after that.

If you ask me if I was in love, I will say to you a resounding yes! And the only thing I thought of after a few days of seeing her was to marry her. Marry? Yes! But I discovered something. What was my discovery, you may ask? I will tell you. I discovered that she was a Christian young lady.

I asked myself, "How is this going to work out between us?" But unknown to me, what was rumbling in my mind was exactly what was rumbling in the mind of my newfound love after she discovered that I was a Muslim. How will I go out with a Muslim, she asked herself?

After we had known each other for less than seven days, I asked her to take me to her parents. I told her that I loved her, and I wanted to marry her.

She asked me, "What did you just say?"

I repeated it to her, "Take me to your family. I am in love with you. I want to marry you!" That was it. After less than two weeks of dating me, she took me to her family.

Do You Love Him?

As we arrived at her village, she introduced me to her parents and openly told them my intentions. Her father called all her uncles and her elder brothers for a meeting with me. It was like a family meeting that was called that very morning.

When we were before her father and all those that had been called to the meeting, and my intention was made known to them, her father turned to her and asked, "Do you love him?"

"Uh … uh … um," she responded.

Her dad said, "I did not ask you to answer me with your nose. I want to hear you answer me with your mouth."

Her father asked again. "Do you love him?"

She replied, "Yes, Daddy."

"Do you want to marry him?"

"Yes, Daddy."

"Alright, that is good," said her father.

Her father asked me where I was from. I replied in the hearing of all her relatives present. Her father asked me to bring my parents to them for further discussion about me marrying his daughter.

Before I left her family home, her father asked me a very notable question. "Do you know that my daughter is a Christian?"

I answered him, "Yes, I know that she is a Christian."

He then told me that he was asking me that question because his daughter told him that I was a practicing Muslim. Even though he had already agreed to let me marry his daughter, he was wondering how it was that I, a Muslim, had come to him to ask for his Christian daughter's hand. He was so surprised. He was thinking that my parents might not accept our coming together in marriage, so he asked that I bring my parents to him.

You see when God is up to something, He knows how to go about it to make His own intentions and purposes come to pass. That was exactly what happened in our own case. Everything began to fall in place as God Himself ordained it to be, all for His Glory!

The Challenge

I told my father about my new-found love and that I wanted to marry her. My father did not object to it. He agreed to it, 100 percent.

He said, "That is good. The Islamic religion has permitted you to marry up to four wives, so there is nothing wrong with that. Where is she from and whose daughter is she?"

I replied that she was from Mangu Local Government Area of Plateau State. I had a wonderful father who was ready to support me in everything, provided what I would do was in accordance with the religion of Islam. He was ready to go with me all the way. He wanted me to be happy.

"But what religion is she from, seeing that people from that area are either Christians, pagans, or idol worshipers," my father asked?

I told him she was a Christian lady.

"So, how are you going to marry her then, knowing you are not a Christian, but a Muslim," my father asked?

I told him that I would convert her to Islam. On hearing that, he was extremely happy and wanted me to go ahead with my intentions. He said he was solidly behind me, even without me discussing with her my intention to convert her from Christianity to the religion of Islam.

Then I started asking myself, "How am I going to do this?"

Changing her from Christianity to Islam would be a challenge for me. After all, I had known this young lady just a few weeks now. What if she refuses to change? That was the question that was so challenging. I felt inside me the courage to tell her — before we married — that I wanted her to become a Muslim. I had shown myself to her family and I wanted to take my father to see her parents to finalize the issue of our wedding.

To my greatest surprise, she agreed to become a Muslim to marry me. I asked her again and she said to me again, "I will become a Muslim."

Right there in my car I asked her to repeat after me the Muslim creed, for a non-Muslim must say it audibly before he or she can become a Muslim or be accepted by Allah. This is called Shahada in Islam, the confession of faith and the first pillar of the Islamic religion, without which all other pillars are of no value. The recitation is uttered repeatedly in the ears of a Muslim newborn infant beginning the day of birth.

It is an Islamic belief that hellfire will not touch anyone who has repeated it, and that by repeating it up to one hundred times a man or woman will be raised up by Allah on the day of resurrection with their faces shining like the moon on the night of its fullness. Right there, I converted her and she became a Muslim, and I changed her name from Damaris to Zainab, a Muslim name.

I then took my father and my uncles to her family and all went well. Within three months of our meeting each other, we married as Muslims.

Living as Husband and Wife

While living together as husband and wife, we enjoyed a blissful marriage life full of love and romance. We never *endured* our marriage. Rather, we enjoyed it to the fullest. Going to the club was a habit that did not end when we married. We could go to a club together and to every place that we used to go before our marriage. We enjoyed ourselves. But we were rooted in a religion that could not bring me face to face with God and His salvation.

My Wife Leaves Me

I loved my new wife, and I knew that she loved me too, but I still believed as a Muslim that I could marry as many as four wives, according to the teaching of Islam. I got an Arabic teacher to teach her Arabic so that she would be able to read the Quran. She was catching up in what she was learning and was true to her newfound faith and religion. The prayers five times a day became a duty to her, since she had to do it as expected of every true Muslim.

Unknown to her I started going out with another lady. That is, it was unknown to her until one day when a friend of my wife came to our house and told her that her husband was cheating on her. At this point the woman in her rose up to investigate me and she did her investigation without me knowing about it. Her investigation revealed the truth and she decided to leave my house and to leave me for good. We woke up one morning and I went to work. She packed her things and left me. And when I came home again, my wife was nowhere to be found.

Jesus Was Working Out My Salvation

My wife never confronted me with her discovery, but she left me because she could not stand her husband going out with another woman. I looked for her from place to place, to no avail. I was made to believe that she was pushed away from my house through diabolical means, and this belief led me to engage the services of an Islamic cleric. The cleric told me that she was pushed out diabolically, and I believed what he said. I believed that because my wife had never told me that I had offended her in any way during our stay together, and I did not know what I had done to her that would make her leave me just like that. The cleric and I engaged in prayer day and night that I would see my wife or learn where she was.

I looked for her for weeks. She went so far away that I thought I would never find her. The cleric and I prayed and recited verses of the Quran day and night and called upon Allah through his prophet. I asked for my wife to come back to me, but there was no answer. There was no answer until, after six months of prayers, Jesus Christ appeared to me.

Jesus Christ Appears to Me

One day I was in my bedroom after the night prayer. I sat down with my counting beads and called upon Allah to come to my aid and bring to me the solution to the predicament that had long troubled me. I was all alone in my house that night. Suddenly, I saw everything very plainly. I saw a man standing in an open field with a mighty building around him and I was standing some distance away from him. The man did not say anything to me, but he was just beckoning me to come to him. He was dressed in white clothing and motioning for me to come to him.

As I was standing there gazing at him, I heard a loud voice from far up in the sky saying to me in English, "This is Jesus. This is Jesus. This is Jesus."

I took a step to go to Him and I saw a ladder descend from the sky to the open field where He was standing. As I moved forward toward Him, He turned and held the ladder and began to climb it. Then, I too held the ladder to follow Him. I opened my eyes and found myself in my bedroom. Behold, this was a dream that appeared to be so real to me! I was with Jesus Christ and I saw Him, face to face. So, I started wondering and pondering, alone in my bedroom.

I had prayed to Allah through Muhammad his prophet for a solution to the situation I found myself in with my wife, but to no avail. And then I saw Jesus beckoning me to come to Him and I heard a loud voice from heaven saying, "This is Jesus. This is Jesus. This is Jesus." What could this dream mean, I kept asking myself? But I could not hear or find an answer within me.

When Day Broke

I waited for the night to be over. At daybreak, I went straight to the cleric who had been standing with me in prayer to Allah for the past six months and told him my revelation, and exactly how I saw Jesus the night before.

Do you know what that scholar said to me? He said, "What that means is that Allah has answered your prayers."

Honestly, I became worried and confused at the same time. Worried and confused because I had been praying to Allah. I had not called the name of Jesus at all. I did not even remember mentioning the name of Jesus once in all my prayers, even though, as a Muslim, I believed in Jesus as a prophet and messenger of Allah who was born of a virgin. Muslims believe His mother was Maryam, the daughter of Imran.

On the other hand, I was so happy to hear that God had answered my prayer that my wife would come back to me. But, many days after my great encounter with Jesus, my wife had not come back on her own. But each time I remembered that I saw the Lord Jesus, I felt an inner peace and an assurance that I would see my wife again. That peace from Jesus encouraged me. Within a month after the encounter I had with Jesus, I found my wife through one of her brothers, who had contacted her friend. Her friend disclosed to us where I would find my wife after seven months of being apart.

Chapter Three

After My Encounter With Jesus

A fter I found my wife, we resumed living together happily. We resolved the differences between us. We resolved them, just the two of us, without anybody coming in to settle it. We also continued in our Islamic religion, and my wife was again very happy in her newfound faith. My wife became content and very committed to our marriage and practicing the religion of Islam and was willing to remain in it until the end of her life, with no intention to go back to Christianity.

'Honey, I Think I Will Go to Church Today'

My wife continued as a converted practicing Muslim and was faithful to the cause, without wavering.

Then, one night, she had a dream, a dream that she was later told was actually a vision. But to her it was a dream that affected her life and brought her to a place of a total turnaround. In her dream, as she narrated, she saw a star in the sky that was very bright in its intensity and at the same time was covered by a thick cloud. The cloud was very dark, but the star was still shining bright amid the cloud. The star turned and took the form of a shining cross. Then, the cross changed and took the form of a person. The person stood and was gazing at her intently without saying a word to her.

But a voice behind Him said, "This is Jesus, the Son of the Most High. This is Jesus, the Son of the Most High. This is Jesus, the Son of the Most High."

And the way that my wife described the voice, I knew it was like the voice that I had heard in my own encounter.

Then, suddenly, the image changed its form into an aircraft, a very big aircraft. She saw the door of the aircraft open, and a ladder come down from it while the aircraft was still suspended, floating between the sky and the earth. And she saw another image at the door of the aircraft. A man was standing there and did not utter a word to her.

But a voice like the former voice said, "This is Gabriel, the angel in His presence. This is Gabriel, the angel in His Presence."

Then she saw people coming, climbing the ladder, and going into the aircraft. People entered en masse and filled the aircraft. When the last person had entered, my wife reached for the ladder, but the ladder rolled back into the aircraft and the door was closed, and she could not enter. Then the aircraft disappeared with all the people that had gone inside it.

She stood there wondering why she was not able to enter the aircraft. She turned around but saw nothing, no one. There were no houses, cars, trees, people — nothing. She was left behind, alone in the world. All she could see at that moment was a vast desert surrounding her. There was nothing she could see. It then dawned on her that she was the only person left in the whole world.

While she was still wondering what had happened, and why it had happened, she heard a voice again. This time the voice sounded very horrifying, like the sound of a terrible thunderstorm.

The voice said to her, "I created you for a purpose. I sent you to planet earth for a purpose, to bring men unto Me, but you chose your own way and, as I said in My own Word, 'Whatever a man sows that shall he reap, whether obedience or disobedience.' For I am a rewarder, and because you have chosen disobedience, your reward for disobedience shall be coming upon you in three seconds. Brimstones of fire shall descend upon you."

Upon hearing those words, she found herself saying, "Lord have mercy and give me another chance. I will do it. I will do your will. Please Lord have mercy. I am so sorry."

As she said those words, she cried and pleaded for mercy. She rolled on the ground and turned, and she looked for something to hold on to, whether a tree, or somebody to help her, but she found none. There were no trees. Nobody. Nothing. She became so afraid, but all she could do was to continue to cry and to beg the Lord for mercy and a second chance to do His will and to fulfill His purpose for creating her.

Then she looked up and saw a huge clock. One second ticked by, and a bell rang loudly. Another second ticked by, and the bell rang again. Then, as a third second was about to tick by, she screamed aloud and woke up, afraid of what she had seen in the encounter.

She was on the bed, crying in her sleep. She woke up crying. Her pillow was wet with tears.

Upon hearing her scream, I woke up and shouted, "Zainab! What is the matter with you?"

She prepared to narrate her experience, but she quickly remembered that her husband was a Muslim. How could she tell me that she saw the Lord Jesus in her sleep? How would I understand her?

When in the house, if she dropped something and she said, "Oh, Jesus," as Christians do, I warned her never to mention that name again. Now, how could she face me and tell me that she saw Jesus? It was a serious problem for her. She decided to tell me only that it was a bad nightmare.

But I insisted on knowing what the bad nightmare was, so that I could see how to make her to stop crying. She told me that she could not remember what the nightmare was, and I believed her, not knowing that she was afraid to tell me that Jesus had spoken to her. She was thinking of what would become of her if she told me the dream she had, knowing that the religion of Islam says, "If a Muslim leaves the faith, he or she has committed a sin against Allah (Riddah, meaning apostasy) and does not deserve to live, but to be killed."

A Muslim believes that if he kills such a person, he is fulfilling the desire of Allah, that it is pleasing to Allah, and that he will be rewarded greatly by Allah. And because she did not want to die, she hid her dream from me and refused to tell me what it was. She thought the only way she could live was to keep what had happened within her.

In the days following, she continued praying the Islamic way, since she had to pray with me whenever I was at home. But she told me later that she really had no peace reciting the Surah Al Fatihah. Instead, she was silently reciting the Lord's Prayer (Our Father, who art in heaven." Matthew 6:9-13). It was the only Christian prayer that she knew how to recite well. She still behaved in the Muslim way, but said the Lord's Prayer, repeating it time after time until I had ended our prayers. I never knew what she was doing. I thought she was in the same spirit with me. I did not know that she had crossed over the fence.

She thought after her encounter that she could hide her experience from me. She was afraid of dying and so pretended to stand with me in a Muslim way and behaved as a Muslim, but prayed silently as a Christian, but she forgot that she could not hide what she was doing from God.

You know what? Two weeks later, something happened one evening while we were having the "lsha" prayer between 7:30 and 7:45 p.m., and she was prayed in her usual, pretentious way. Later she would tell me that as her head was on the ground and she was appearing to pray in the Islamic way, she heard the voice of the Lord.

And the Lord said to her, "You hypocrite. How long shall you continue in this way? If you die now, you are still not saved. Come out from among them and be ye separated."

She was shocked. She asked me after the evening prayer, "Did you speak to me during the prayer?"

I said, "No! How could I have spoken to you when you know it is not right for a Muslim to say anything outside the recitation of the Surah Al Fatihah when praying?"

I asked if anything was wrong. She told me she heard someone say something, but she was afraid to tell me what she had heard.

Later that night, she fell into a trance. While she was half asleep, she saw a pit of fire and a multitude of people trooping into it. A force kept pushing her towards the fire, but when she opened her eyes, she saw nothing. This continued for a week and it was giving her serious headaches because she could not sleep well. But she did not stop her life of hypocrisy of religion, because she was afraid to die. This kept her restless for days.

The situation kept her off-sides with God. She did not recognize that only He has the power to shape the life and destiny of man, and He does so as He pleases.

Night after night, she continued to see the fire in that pit, and night after night, the situation was unknown to me. I was sleeping well each night, but my wife was almost constantly awake because of the fire that appeared before her. In the second week, she started visualizing the fire not just at night, but also in the day. This vision was no longer in her dreams but in her waking life.

Sometimes, when she was walking on the street, she saw the fire in front of her. It would disappear and come again several times. She became even more restless and felt that she was almost going insane.

Then it dawned on her that she *would* soon become insane if she continued pretending to be a Muslim, and she continued to be tortured day after day, night after night, by the sight of that fiery pit. And the husband that she feared would still be alive and enjoying his life. She thought that no one would listen to her story.

But then she realized, of God and man, who should she fear? She made up her mind to obey the voice of God. She would face the music, no matter what the outcome. After all these hallucinating experiences, she decided to talk with me and face the consequences.

The next morning, as I readied for work, my wife said, "Honey, please, can we talk?"

"What are we talking about this time?"

She said, "Honey, I think I will be going to church today."

I was shocked, and said, "What did you just say?"

She repeated herself — this time with some boldness.

I became angry and retorted, "Haven't I asked you not to say that word (church) again? In fact, you must be joking. I don't ever want to hear that word again in this house, and if you try it, I will make sure I kill you!" I said those horrible words to the wife I love.

She said, "Well, I am not asking for permission from you. I am only informing you of what I will do — in case you come back from work and do not see me at home."

I said to her, "Don't try it." I picked up my car keys and left for work.

That day was truly her day for a divine turn-around. She was left alone, with her mind made up to go to church. She went to church that day and confessed Jesus Christ as the Savior of her soul. This was the encounter my wife had that led her to give her heart to the Lord Jesus Christ. She received Jesus as her Lord and personal Savior, which is a long story that she details in her book, titled *Isn't God Awesome.*[1]

---

[1] Damaris Zainab Isah, *Isn't God Awesome* (2nd edition), CreateSpace Independent Publishing Platform, September 5, 2018, https://www. amazon.com/Isnt-Awesome-Damaris-Zainab-Isah/dp/1726375641#ace-7448806443.

Chapter Four

I Now Know the Truth

M y wife had become a committed Christian and was attending church regularly. She became so serious about it that there was no service or program in the church that she did not attend. This became very tough for me. The woman that I brought to Islam was now a Christian and she was going to church. It was tough because my family members were aware of it, and they were against it. They asked me to divorce her without delay.

But I loved my wife. Divorcing her was not the solution. I said to them that I brought her to Islam not by my own power, but by Allah's willing, and I will bring her back again. Friend, unknown to me, Jesus saved her soul to be an instrument for my own salvation.

'Honey, Please Can You Drive Me to the Crusade Ground?'

One day my wife came home from church with an invitation to attend a church crusade at another church far away from where we lived at the time. It was a three-day crusade, an open-air meeting.

She asked me, "Honey, please, can you drive me to the crusade ground?" She showed me the flier. When I noticed it was a church event, I wanted to refuse to take her, but deep down inside of me I felt an urge to drive her to the place.

All I said to her was, "Where is the venue of the program?"

And when the day came, I drove her there. As she left the car, I said to her, "I will not wait for you here. I will drive down to my family house to stay, after which I will come back to pick you up after you finish at the crusade ground."

The program was to start at 5:30 p.m., and she asked me to return at 11 p.m., so we could go back home together. I drove her the first night to the place, and then the second night, too. On the third night of the crusade, I decided to wait for her at the crusade ground, which was in front of a church auditorium of the ministry that had invited her. Across from the place there was a railroad track. I parked our car by the railroad track, and I sat on the trunk of the car, and watched and listened to the preacher's sermon.

The preacher's sermon was about the arrest, crucifixion, death, and the resurrection of Jesus Christ. He demonstrated how Jesus was crucified on the cross, shed His blood on the cross, died on that same cross, was buried, and rose from the dead on the third day. He kept on preaching about how Jesus Christ, the Prince of Peace, rose from the dead by the Spirit of the Living God, and He was taken into Heaven by the same Holy Spirit. The statements of the preacher got my rapt attention.

You could sum up the sermon by saying that the preacher was pointing the people to the fact that Jesus is the Prince of Peace. "Only when you receive Him will you find peace here on the earth. He is the only begotten Son of God!"

As a Muslim, I started thinking of what the Quran says about Jesus. I was thinking and listening to the preacher and at the same time my Muslim beliefs came to mind. Muslims believe that when the Roman soldiers came to arrest Jesus for crucifixion, Allah put the image of Jesus on the face of one of the Jews, and the Jew was crucified instead of Jesus Christ, a messenger of Allah. Then Allah took Jesus to heaven, unhurt. Allah substituted Him with someone else for crucifixion.

Quran 4:157, 158

"And because of their saying: We slew the Messiah, Jesus son of Mary, Allah's messenger — they slew him not nor crucified him, but it appeared so unto them; and lo! those who disagree concerning it are in doubt thereof; they have no knowledge thereof save pursuit of a conjecture; they slew him not for certain. But Allah took him up unto Himself. Allah was ever Mighty, Wise."[2]

I asked myself these vital questions: If Allah is God and all-powerful, why must he deceive his creature to save his messenger by placing the image of Jesus on an innocent man? Why must he violate the words in the Quran said to quote Jesus himself?

Quran 19:33

"Peace on me the day I was born, and the day I die, and the day I shall be raised alive!"

---

[2] All quotations from the Quran are from the English translation by Mohammed Marmaduke Pickthall (http://www.ishwar.com/islam/holy_quran_%28pickthall%29/).

The Jews said, "We slew the Messiah, Jesus, son of Mary." (Quran 4:157). The Muslims say Jesus did not die at all! But in the Quran, Jesus said, "The day I die." (Quran 19:33).

With these verses in mind, I continued to think, "We slew Jesus." Jesus said, "The day He shall die." Quran 4:158 said that "Allah took him up unto Himself." But the phrases "we slew him," "I die," and "Allah took him up unto Himself," all indicate that Jesus died, was raised from the dead, and was taken up to Allah alive. Because Jesus said, "The day I die, and the day I shall be raised alive!"

And Allah said in Quran 3:55, "(And remember) when Allah said: O Jesus! Lo! I am gathering thee and causing thee to ascend unto me."

These verses came to mind when the man of God was preaching. The preacher said emphatically, "The Prince of Peace rose from the dead and is alive today." Prince of Peace?

Quran 19:33

Jesus said, "Peace on me the day I was born, and the day I die, and the day I shall be raised alive!"

I saw miracles performed through the name of Jesus on that ground. A deaf and dumb little girl heard and spoke. A young deaf boy heard with his ears through prayer in the name of Jesus Christ. I left the place with what I heard and saw. At the altar call — a call for those who want to give their hearts to the Lord Jesus and receive Him as their Lord and Savior to step forward — I did not respond. I hardened my heart. But inside I knew that something had happened to me.

After that night I could not perform ablution to pray in an Islamic way. I picked up my Quran and picked up my wife's Good News Bible and began to read the Bible side by side with the Quran, just to know the truth about what I heard at the crusade ground. This went on for three weeks. I gave my attention to nothing but the reading of the Bible and the Quran every morning, noon, and night, making my research to know if what I had heard preached was the truth.

I Discover the Truth

As I was going through the pages of the Bible, reading, and meditating on what I had read, I discovered the truth of what the Quran says about Jesus Christ of the Bible. But what the Muslim clerics interpret as they preach does not agree with the Quran, even though it is clearly written therein. Instead of following the truth about Jesus, the Muslims believed much more about the life of the prophet Muhammad in place of what the Quran says concerning Jesus Christ.

It is believed in Islam that each aspect of the life of the prophet Mohammad exemplifies his perfection and is of value for those who seek a model of guidance, because his life was specifically designed by Allah for this purpose. They believed that all of the prophet's attributes, virtues, and qualities had been showered on him as gifts from Allah. This brought the conclusion to them that there is no one like Muhammad. The religion of Islam presented it thus, that Allah has been the one who designed all the physical features, the style of living, and the conduct of the prophet in such a perfect manner and made him to be the savior of all mankind.

Therefore, most Muslims believe that each quality of the prophet Muhammad's life serves as an expression for the glory and grandeur of Allah. He was said to be the perfect and sinless prophet of Allah. But the Quran declares that Jesus Christ, the son of Mary, is the greatest of all the prophets, not Muhammad, and that only Jesus, not Muhammad, is without sin.

Quran 2:252, 253

These are the portents of Allah which We recite unto thee (Muhammad) with truth, and lo! thou art of the number of

(Our) messengers; Of those messengers, some of whom We have caused to excel others, and of whom there are some unto whom Allah spoke, while some of them He exalted (above others) in degree; and We gave Jesus, son of Mary, clear proofs (of Allah's Sovereignty) and We supported him with the holy Spirit. And if Allah had so willed it, those who followed after them would not have fought one with another after the clear proofs had come unto them. But they differed, some of them believing and some disbelieving. And if Allah had so willed it, they would not have fought one with another; but Allah doeth what He will.

In the verses above, Jesus Christ is the one whom Allah caused to excel over all other prophets. He was the one who was exalted above all other prophets. He was the only one who was given clear proofs and was also supported with the Holy Spirit. Clearly these made Jesus Christ the greatest of all the prophets. The Holy Bible says of Jesus Christ:

Matthew 12:41-42

The men of Nineveh shall rise up in judgment with this generation and

*condemn it, because they repented at
the preaching of Jonah; and indeed, a
greater than Jonah is here. The queen of
the South shall rise up in judgment with
this generation and condemn it, for she
came from the ends of the earth to hear
the wisdom of Solomon; and indeed a
greater than Solomon is here.*[3]

Even John the Baptist, whom the Quran also
recognizes as a prophet, specifically and categor-
ically made it clear that Jesus is the greatest and
mightiest of all the prophets.

Luke 3:15-17

*Now as the people were in expectation,
and all reasoned in their hearts about
John, whether he was the Christ or not,
John answered, saying to all, "I indeed
baptize you with water; but one mightier
than I is coming, whose sandal strap I
am not worthy to loose. He will baptize
you with the Holy Spirit and fire. His
winnowing fan is in his hand, and He*

---

will thoroughly clean out His threshing floor, and gather the wheat into His barn; but the chaff He will burn with unquenchable fire."

The Sinlessness of the Prophets

Is Muhammad a sinless prophet? The following verses of the Quran below give the answer to whether he was sinless or not. Quran 53:2 indicates that he has no sin: *"Your comrade (Muhammad) erreth not, nor is deceived."*

The word 'erreth' means to make a mistake, to sin, or to stray. This verse says he has not sinned. But other verses of the same Quran indicate that Muhammad *had* sinned. What a contradiction! The verse above says he has committed no sin. But in the verses below from the Quran, Muhammad is told to ask forgiveness for the sin he committed.

Quran 40:55

Then have patience (O Muhammad). Lo! The promise of Allah is true. And ask forgiveness of thy sin, and hymn the praise of thy Lord at fall of night and in the early hours.

Quran 48:1–2

Lo! We have given thee (O Muhammad) a signal victory, that Allah may forgive thee of thy sin that which is past and that which is to come, and may perfect his favor unto thee, and may guide thee on a right path.

Not only was he to ask for his sins to be forgiven, but he was also to look for the perfection of favor and guidance on the right path to follow. So, the question is, how can a prophet who was also looking for the forgiveness of his past, present, and future sin become the savior of mankind? How can someone who was looking for the perfection of favor, and looking for guidance, be able to perfect others and guide others to follow on the right path?

Quran 47:19

So know (O Muhammad) that there is no God save Allah, and ask forgiveness for thy sin and for believing men and believing women, Allah knoweth (both) your place of turmoil and your place of rest.

These verses clearly show that Muhammad was not a sinless prophet, but rather he was to ask for the forgiveness of his own sin and the forgiveness of the sins of other men and women that the Quran claimed he was to save. The following is a synthesis of his personal prayer found in Sahih Buhari Volume 8:335, 337, 407, and 408.

In the night's stillness, far from the crowd and alone by himself and the thoughts of his heart, he prays confessing the truth he knows within his soul: "Oh God, I acknowledge and confess before You all my sins. Please forgive them, as no one can forgive sins except You. Forgive my mistakes, those done intentionally, or out of ignorance; forgive my sins of the past, present and the future, which I did openly or secretly. Forgive the wrong I have done, jokingly or seriously. I seek your protection from all the evil I have done. Wash away my sins and cleanse my heart from all the sins as a white garment is cleansed from the filth, and let there be a great distance between me and my sins, as you made the East and West far from each other."

This is a prayer that expressed a heart that understood the depth of sin in the soul. The prayer acknowledges a nature within that is bent toward sin. And it reflects the desire to cleanse that depth of sin. This is the prayer of a man quite struggling with sin. He asks forgiveness for his past, present, and future sins, because he knew that as a normal man, he was going to sin. It is inevitable for him to sin, so he asked for forgiveness for the things he had done or would do. He asked forgiveness for mistakes and sins, those done intentionally or unintentionally.

He knows that the sins he committed are "evil" and confessed that to God. He does not make light of his sins. The sins he committed are "filth" in God's eyes. This prayer was prayed by Muhammad. Clearly, he knew he was a sinner. He made this confession public repeatedly. He himself stated he was a sinner. Yet many Muslims today say that he was not a sinner. They claim he is the only prophet who never committed any sin. He is referred today by the Muslims as the holiest of all the prophets.

Quran 53:1, 2

> *By the star when it setteth, your comrade (Muhammad) erreth not, nor is deceived ...*

The Quran says he has not sinned. Yet he prayed the prayer above for the forgiveness of his sins? I want you to think about this!

The Sinlessness of Jesus Christ

Jesus Christ was and is the perfect of all the prophets. He knew no sin, neither has He committed any sin. He, in His perfection, has never asked God for the forgiveness of His sin because He has never committed any. Rather you will only see that Jesus asked for the forgiveness of the sins of others in His humanity and He pronounced forgiveness of the sins of others in His Divinity. Because only God, who knew no sin, can forgive the sins of those who have committed sin. In asking for the forgiveness of others, Jesus said in Luke 23:34,

> *Then Jesus said, "Father, forgive them, for they know not what they do."*

In forgiving the sins of another, Jesus said in Luke 5:20:

> *When he saw their faith, he said to him, "Man, your sins are forgiven you."*

The Quran also declares that Jesus Christ is faultless (sinless).

Quran 19:16–21

And make mention of Mary in the scripture, when she had withdrawn from her people to a chamber looking east, and had chosen seclusion from them. Then We sent unto her Our Spirit and it assumed for her the likeness of a perfect man. She said: Lo! I seek refuge in the Beneficent one and from thee, if thou art God-fearing. He said: I am only a messenger of thy Lord, that I may bestow on thee a faultless son.

The Bible also revealed the sinlessness of Jesus Christ, as Jesus says in John 8:45–46,

"But because I tell the truth, you do not believe Me. Which of you convicts Me of sin? And if I tell the truth, why do you not believe Me?"

And in 1st Peter 2:21–24:

For to this you were called, because Christ also suffered for us, leaving us an example, that you should follow His steps: "Who committed no sin, Nor was deceit found in His mouth;" who, when

*He was reviled, did not revile in return;
when He suffered, He did not threaten,
but committed Himself to Him who
judges righteously; who Himself bore
our sins in His own body on the tree,
that we, having died to sins, might live
for righteousness—by whose stripes you
were healed.*

Isaiah 53:9

*And they made His grave with the
wicked—but with the rich at His death,
because He had done no violence, nor
was any deceit in His mouth.*

1st John 3:5

*And you know that He was manifested to
take away our sins, and in Him is no sin.*

Hebrews 4:15

*For we do not have a High Priest who
cannot sympathize with our weaknesses,
but was in all points tempted as we are,
yet without sin.*

Hebrews 7:25–26

*Therefore He is also able to save to
the uttermost those who come to God*

*through Him, since He always lives to
make intercession for them. For such
a High Priest was fitting for us, who is
holy, harmless, undefiled, separate from
sinners, and has become higher than
the heavens ...*

2nd Corinthians 5:21

*For He made Him who knew no sin to
be sin for us, that we might become the
righteousness of God in Him.*

These are a few of the numerous verses in the
Bible that declare to us that Jesus Christ lived a
sinless life upon the earth. This qualifies Him to
be the Savior of mankind. These are the scriptures that brought me to know the truth about
the sinlessness of Jesus Christ, and to know that
Muhammad, being a man of sin, cannot and will
not be the savior of any mortal man.

Chapter Five

I Am Convicted
to Be a Christian

A s I continued in my quest to discover the truth in the course of my study, I became convicted to give my heart to the Lord Jesus Christ to accept Him as my Lord and my Savior. The truth I discovered in verses of the Quran and the Bible became so real in me that I knew that following Jesus Christ was the right way for me. Verses of the Quran convicted me to become a Christian more and more. The more I read the Quran, the more I see the truth that brings me face to face with the person of Jesus Christ as my Savior. And the more I read the Bible, the more I see the verses of the Bible confirming to me what the Quran says about Jesus being the only way of Salvation. For instance:

Quran 3:113, 114

> *They are not all alike. Of the People of the Scripture there is a staunch community who recite the revelations of Allah in the night season, falling prostrate (before Him). They believe in Allah and the Last Day, and enjoin right conduct and forbid indecency, and vie one with another in good works. These are of the righteous.*

The Quran refers to followers of Jesus Christ (that is the Christians) as "people of the scripture" or "people of the Book." The Quran says in the verses above that they are of the righteous. So, if the Quran says that Christians or followers of Jesus Christ are of the righteous, why do Muslims reject what the Quran is saying, that Christians are righteous? The Quran also says that the followers of Jesus Christ are the believers.

Quran 3:53

> *Our lord! We believe in that which thou hast revealed and we follow him whom thou has sent (Jesus Christ). Enroll us among those who witness (to the truth).*

Muhammad is the one who turned the heart of his followers to hate the Christians! Look at this verse:

Quran 3:26–28

Say: O Allah! Owner of Sovereignty! Thou givest sovereignty unto whom Thou wilt, and Thou withdrawest sovereignty from whom Thou wilt. Thou exaltest whom Thou wilt, and Thou abasest whom Thou wilt. In Thy hand is the good. Lo! Thou art Able to do all things. Thou causest the night to pass into the day, and Thou causest the day to pass into the night. And Thou bringest forth the living from the dead, and Thou bringest forth the dead from the living. And Thou givest sustenance to whom Thou choosest, without stint. Let not the believers take disbelievers for their friends in preference to believers. Whoso doeth that hath no connection with Allah unless (it be) that ye but guard yourselves against them, taking (as it were) security. Allah biddeth you beware (only) of Himself. Unto Allah is the journeying.

You see, Quran 3:113 says Christians (followers of Christ) are the righteous and not the disbelievers, but in this verse, Muslims are told not to take the Christians as their friends. The same Quran says, "Allah has set the followers of Jesus above those who are not His followers" in the verse below.

Quran 3:55

(And remember) when Allah said: O Jesus! Lo! I am gathering thee and causing thee to ascend unto Me, and am cleansing thee of those who disbelieve and am setting those who follow thee above those who disbelieve until the Day of Resurrection. Then unto Me ye will (all) return, and I shall judge between you as to that wherein ye used to differ.

This also shows that the Quran contradicts itself calling the Christians believers and now disbelievers, if referring to Christians.

Quran 3:68

Lo! Those of mankind who have the best claim to Abraham are those who followed him, and this Prophet (Jesus Christ) and those who believe (with him) (the

Christians); and Allah is the protecting guardian of the believers (the Christians).

The Quran says that Allah is the protective guardian of the followers of Jesus Christ (that is the Christians). Muhammad said Muslims who are the followers of Allah should not be friends of the Christians. This sounds contradictory to what the Quran says concerning the Christians!

The Divinity of Jesus Christ

Furthermore, I found it to be true what Christians profess concerning the divinity of Jesus Christ, while the Muslims stand in opposition to the claims of the Christians about the divinity of the Lord Jesus Christ. The Quran says that John the Baptist came to confirm a word from Allah.

Quran 3:39

And the angels called to him (Zachariah) as he stood praying in the sanctuary: Allah giveth thee glad tidings of (a son whose name is) John, (who cometh) to confirm a word from Allah lordly, chaste, a prophet of the righteous.

John the Baptist was sent by God to confirm a word from Allah, which shall stand to be Lordly, chaste, and a prophet of the righteous. This is the claim of the Christians and is revealed in the Bible concerning John the Baptist.

Isaiah 40:3

The voice of one crying in the wilderness: "Prepare the way of the Lord; Make straight in the desert a highway for our God."

Matthew 3:3

For this is he who was spoken of by the prophet Isaiah, saying: "The voice of one crying in the wilderness: Prepare the way of the Lord; Make His paths straight."

Matthew 11:10

For this is he of whom it is written: "Behold, I send My messenger before Your face, Who will prepare Your way before You."

Both the Quran and the Holy Bible authenticate the prophecy of John the Baptist about the coming of the Lord Jesus Christ, that He was coming from God Himself.

Quran 3:42–45

> *And when the angels said O Mary Lo! Allah hath chosen thee and made thee pure, and preferred thee above (all) the women of creation. O Mary! Be obedient to thy Lord, prostrate thyself and bow with those who bow (in worship). This is of the tidings of things hidden. We reveal it unto thee (Muhammad). Thou wast not present with them when they threw their pens (to know) which of them should be the guardian of Mary, nor wast thou present with them when they quarrel (there upon). (And remember) when the angels said: O Mary Allah giveth thee glad tidings of a word from Him, whose name is the Messiah, Jesus, Son of Mary, illustrious in the world and the Hereafter, and one of those brought near (unto Allah).*

These verses reveal to us that Jesus Christ proceeded from God as a word from Allah and that he was one of those brought near to Allah. This tells me that the divinity of Jesus Christ is unquestionable to those who open their hearts to receive what God revealed concerning Jesus Christ. The Lordship of Christ is established in the fact that He (Jesus Christ) is a word from Him.

Quran 3:46–50

He will speak unto mankind in his cradle and in his manhood, and he is of the righteous. She said: My Lord! How can I have a child when no mortal hath touched me? He said: So (it will be). Allah createth what He will. If He decreeth a thing, He saith unto it only: Be! and it is. And He will teach him the Scripture and wisdom, and the Torah and the Gospel, And will make him a messenger unto the Children of Israel, (saying): Lo! I come unto you with a sign from your Lord. Lo! I fashion for you out of clay the likeness of a bird, and I breathe into it and it is a bird, by Allah's leave. I heal him who was born blind, and the leper, and I raise the dead, by Allah's leave. And I announce unto you what ye eat and what ye store up in your houses. Lo! herein verily is a portent for you, if ye are to be believers. And (I come) confirming that which was before me of the Torah, and to make lawful some of that which was forbidden unto you. I come unto you with a sign from your Lord, so keep your duty to Allah and obey me.

The sign that Jesus spoke about here is a sign that was not given to any of the prophets that came before Him. It was given to Him alone. He came with this sign from the Lord as a portent word that proceeded from God Himself. Jesus Christ performed miracles, signs, and wonders that no other prophet performed. He was approved by God like no other.

Acts 2:22

Men of Israel, hear these words: Jesus of Nazareth, a Man attested by God to you by miracles, wonders, and signs which God did through Him in your midst, as you yourselves also know ...

If humanity can believe and come to the knowledge of what God said and revealed concerning Jesus Christ, then we will understand that there is no basis for anybody to doubt the truth about Jesus proceeding from God for the Salvation of mankind. Even the Quran stated that Muhammad was instructed by Allah to ask those who read the scriptures (the Christians) that were before him if he was in doubt, and that the truth about Jesus Christ is in what they have read, and it is that same truth from his Lord that came unto him.

Quran 10:94–95

And if thou (Muhammad) art in doubt concerning that which We revealed unto thee [about Jesus Christ], then question those who read the Scripture [the Bible] (that was) before thee. Verily the truth from thy Lord hath come unto thee [in it]. So be not thou of the waverers. And be not thou of those who deny the revelations of Allah, for then wert thou of the losers.

The truth is in what was revealed to Muhammad concerning Jesus Christ! And he was enjoined by Allah in the verse above not to deny or disbelieve the revelation that was revealed. To deny that which was revealed to him would make him to be of the losers. Furthermore, if Muhammad was in doubt of what was revealed, he should ask questions of the Christians who read the truth (which is the Torah and the Injil) that came before him. The truth is in what they read, as I stated above. This is awesome!

Jesus Is Christ the Word of God and the Spirit of God

Both the Holy Bible and the Quran laid bare that the Lord Jesus Christ is the very Word of God and the Spirit of God. Denying these facts placed one as an individual among the losers or among the unbelieving, according to:

Quran 10:95

And be not thou of those who doubt the revelations of Allah, for then wert thou of the losers.

In the Bible, in Matthew:10 32–33, Jesus said,

Therefore whoever confesses Me before men, him I will also confess before My Father who is in heaven. But whoever denies Me before men, him I will also deny before My Father who is in heaven.

The Quran has this to say concerning Jesus being the Word of God and the Spirit of God:

Quran 3:42–53

And when the angels said: O Mary! Lo! Allah hath chosen thee and made thee pure, and hath preferred thee above (all) the women of creation. O Mary! Be obedient to thy Lord, prostrate thyself and bow with those who bow (in worship). This is of the tidings of things hidden. We reveal it unto thee (Muhammad). Thou wast not present with them when they threw their pens (to know) which of them should be the guardian of Mary, nor wast thou present with them when they quarreled (thereupon). (And remember) when the angels said: O Mary! Lo! Allah giveth thee glad tidings of a word from him, whose name is the Messiah, Jesus, son of Mary, illustrious in the world and the Hereafter, and one of those brought near (unto Allah). He will speak unto mankind in his cradle and in his manhood, and he is of the righteous. She said: My Lord! How can I have a child when no mortal hath touched me? He said: So (it will be). Allah createth what He will. If He decreeth a thing, He saith unto it only: Be! and it is. And He will teach him the Scripture and wisdom, and the Torah and the Gospel, And will make him a messenger unto the Children of Israel, (saying): Lo! I come unto you with a sign from your Lord. Lo!

I fashion for you out of clay the likeness of a bird, and I breathe into it and it is a bird, by Allah's leave. I heal him who was born blind, and the leper, and I raise the dead, by Allah's leave. And I announce unto you what ye eat and what ye store up in your houses. Lo! herein verily is a portent for you, if ye are to be believers. And (I come) confirming that which was before me of the Torah, and to make lawful some of that which was forbidden unto you. I come unto you with a sign from your Lord, so keep your duty to Allah and obey me. Lo! Allah is my Lord and your Lord, so worship Him. That is a straight path. But when Jesus became conscious of their disbelief, he cried: Who will be my helpers in the cause of Allah? The disciples said: We will be Allah's helpers. We believe in Allah, and bear thou witness that we have surrendered (unto Him). Our Lord! We believe in that which Thou hast revealed and we follow him whom Thou hast sent. Enroll us among those who witness (to the truth).

These verses of the Quran above confirm to mankind the authority of Jesus Christ as the eternal Word of God and the eternal Spirit of God. The Quran declared Jesus as a "Word from Us" and a "Spirit from Us." This means He is the word of Allah and the spirit of Allah, if the Arabic name for Allah is the literal word translated into English as God. Then it can be written literally as a word from God, or to write that verse as literally as it came, it can be written as "Jesus Christ the Word of God" and "Jesus Christ the Spirit of God." As the Quran says: Isa Kalimatullah (which means Jesus the Word of God) and Isa Ruhallah (which means Jesus the Spirit of God).

Jesus Christ came as a Word of God and illustrious in the world and in the hereafter. The word illustrious is an adjective that means dignified. The Quran says of Jesus, His name is called the Messiah, Jesus, Son of Mary, dignified in the world and in heaven (which is the hereafter). Jesus Christ as a Spirit from God came with a sign that enabled Him to create what He wants to create, heal whom He wants to heal, deliver whom He wants to deliver, and raise from the dead whom He wants to raise from the dead, as indicated above.

These divine attributes are found only in God Himself, and they are attributed to and found in Jesus Christ. A Word from God is not in any way different from God because that Word proceeded from God Himself. A Spirit from God is also not in any way different from God because the same Spirit proceeds from God. This means the Word from God, or the Word of God is God! And the Spirit from God or the Spirit of God is God! Furthermore, the Trinity is established in the Quran: Allah Himself, a Word from Him (Allah), and the Spirit from Him (Allah).

Quran 66:12

And Mary, daughter of 'Imran, whose body was chaste, therefor We breathed therein something of Our Spirit. And she put faith in the Words of her lord and His scriptures, and was of the obedient.

Quran 19:16–22

And make mention of Mary in the scripture, when she had withdrawn from her people to a chamber looking East. And had chosen seclusion from them. Then We sent unto her Our Spirit and it assumed for her the likeness of a perfect man. She said: Lo! I seek refuge in the Beneficent One from thee, if thou art God-fearing. He said: I am only a messenger of thy Lord, that I may bestow on thee a faultless son. She said: How can I have a son when no mortal hath touched me,

neither have I been unchaste? He said: So
(it will be). Thy Lord saith: It is easy for
me. And (it will be) that We may make
of him a revelation for mankind and a
mercy from Us and it is a thing ordained.
And she conceived him, and she withdrew
with him to a far place.

In different places in the verses above, we find the words 'We,' 'Our,' and 'Us.' Who do these words refer to? God cannot and will not associate Himself with any of His creatures. In His divinity, He stands to be God alone. Far be it from God to associate Himself with any other thing or being beside Himself. But here God, even in the Quran, is making reference with the words 'We,' 'Our,' and 'Us.' This indicates that associated with God are His Word with Him and His Spirit with Him. He Himself is Himself — if I may use this phrase. His Word is He Himself and His Spirit is He Himself. God, Word, and Spirit are one in one God. They are inseparable. They all agree in one! God partners in sovereignty only with Himself.

Quran 18:111

And say praise Allah, who hath not taken
unto Himself a son, and who hath no
partner in the sovereignty, nor with any

protecting friend through dependence.
And magnify Himself with magnificence.

What this verse says is the claim of all Muslims. Yet, spread in different verses of the Quran I saw Allah partnering Himself in sovereignty. Thus, those words 'We,' 'Our,' and 'Us' are found written there. He partners with his Word and His Spirit in Sovereignty.

Quran 76:28

We, even We created them, and strengthened their frame. And when We will, We can replace them, bringing others like them in their state.

Genesis 1:26–27

Then God said, "Let Us make man in Our image, according to Our likeness, let them have dominion over the fish of the sea, over the birds of the air, and over the cattle, over all the earth and over every creeping thing that creeps on the earth." So God created man in His own image, in the image of God He created him, male and female He created them.

Quran 2:35

And We said: O Adam! Dwell thou and thy wife in the garden, and eat ye freely (of the fruits) there of where ye will; but come not nigh this tree lest ye become wrong doers.

Look at that verse carefully. He did not say, "I said." It is written, "We said." This indicates that more than one personality was talking to Adam. The person of Allah, His Word, and His Spirit are the 'we' that were talking to Adam: one in three! The Quranic Trinity is confirmed in various verses of the Quran. Knowing this will make anyone who reads the Quran with understanding accept the Oneness of Allah manifesting Himself through His Word and His Spirit. Thus, He makes Himself to be three in one and one in three, yet He is only one God.

Jesus Christ, the Word of God and the Spirit of God, in the Bible

1st John 5:6–8

This is He who came by water and blood — Jesus Christ; not only by water, but by water and blood. And it is the Spirit who bears witness, because the Spirit is truth.

> *For there are three that bear witness in heaven: the Father, the Word, and the Holy Spirit; and these three are one. And there are three that bear witness on earth: the Spirit, the water, and the blood; and these three agree as one.*

Before God sent Jesus into the world to dwell among men, the Word and the Spirit were in heaven with the Father, bearing record of all the activities going on in heaven. Thus, the Father, the Word, and the Holy Spirit are seen to be one God in heaven because these three agree in one. The Quran confirms what the Bible presented to us.

Quran 4:171

> *... Jesus son of Mary was only a messenger of Allah, and his word which he conveyed unto Mary, and a spirit from Him. ...*

The phrase Jesus is a "word ... and a spirit from Him" is a confirmation of what the Bible says above, for there are three that bear record in heaven; the Father, the Word, and the Holy Spirit. The same Word and Spirit Allah sent unto Mary was recorded in the Bible.

Luke1:26–35

Now in the sixth month the angel Gabriel was sent by God to a city of Galilee named Nazareth, to a virgin betrothed to a man whose name was Joseph, of the house of David. The virgin's name was Mary. And having come in, the angel said to her, "Rejoice, highly favored one, the Lord is with you; blessed are you among women!" But when she saw Him, she was troubled at his saying, and considered what manner of greeting this was. Then the angel said to her, "Do not be afraid, Mary, for you have found favor with God. And behold, you will conceive in your womb and bring forth a Son, and shall call his name Jesus. He will be great, and will be called the Son of the Highest; and the Lord God will give Him the throne of His father David. And he shall reign over the house of Jacob forever; and of his kingdom there shall be no end. Then Mary said to the angel, "How can this be, since I do not know a man?" And the angel answered and said to her, "The Holy Spirit will come upon you, and the power of the Highest will overshadow you; therefore, also, that Holy One who is to be born will be called the Son of God."

A Word from Us and a Spirit from Us is stated in:

Quran 3:42, 45

And when the angels said: O Mary! Lo! Allah hath chosen thee and made thee pure, and hath preferred thee above (all) the women of creation. (And remember) when the angel said: O Mary! Lo! Allah giveth thee glad tidings of a word from Him whose name is the Messiah, Jesus, son of Mary, illustrious in the world and in the Hereafter, and one of those brought near (unto Allah).

Quran 66:12

And Mary, daughter of 'Imran, whose body was chaste, therefore We breathed therein something of our spirit. And she put faith in the words of her Lord and His scriptures, and was of the obedient.

Quran 19:19

He said: I am only a messenger of thy Lord, that I may bestow on thee a faultless son.

Quran 21:91

And she who was chaste, therefore We breathed into her something of our spirit and made her and her son a token for (all) peoples.

This confirms that Jesus Christ is indeed the very Word of God and the Spirit of God. No person should doubt the infallibility of the revealed Word of God. Rather, what God revealed is to be believed, rather than any falsehood or doctrine of men. Jesus is truly one of the three that agree in one because He is the Word of God and the Spirit of God Himself. He is the Word and the Spirit of the living God personified. He was there with God, even before the beginning. He is one with God, and God used Him to create all things.

John 1:1–3

In the beginning was the Word, and the Word was with God, and the Word was God. He was in the beginning with God. All things where made through Him, and without Him nothing was made that was made.

Furthermore, the equality of Jesus Christ in Divinity with God is made sure. God spoke His

Word (Jesus) and He created all things that are in the invisible world and the visible world.

Hebrews 11:3

By faith we understand that the worlds were framed by the word of God, so that the things which are seen were not made of things which are visible.

John 1:10, 14

He was in the world, and the world was made through Him, and the world did not know Him. ... And the Word became flesh and dwelt among us, and we beheld His glory, the glory as of the only begotten of the Father, full of grace and truth.

Quran 50:38

And verily We created the heavens and the earth, and all that is between them, in six days, and naught of weariness touched Us.

These are unquestionable facts about the person of Jesus Christ that place Him in the class of God and reveal to mankind His divinity as God and Creator of the heavens and the earth, and all that is therein! These are the facts that convicted me to become a Christian, facts that stood out and facts with authority of which is confirmed in the Bible. The very word of God in the writings of John, which were in existence 600 years before the Quran, can save our souls from the uprising of false doctrines.

The author, Isah Jesse Abraham, with his wife, Damaris
Zainab Isah, his son Abdul'azzeez Joseph Isah, who was
nine years old, and his daughter Sharon Sa'adatu Isah,
who was one year old. The photo was taken at Maiduguri
Borno State Nigeria.

The author, Isah Jesse Abraham, and his wife, Damaris Zainab Isah, with the body of their son, Abdul'azzeez Joseph Isah. He was ten years old when he was killed on September 1, 2000. Days later, several men who belong to the Islamic faith told them that their son had been killed as a warning to them for leaving the Islamic faith for the Christian faith. No one was charged with his death.

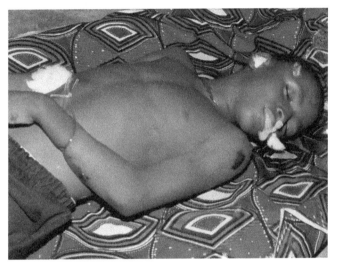

The body of Abdul'azzez Joseph Isah rests in a mortuary at Jalingo, Taraba State, Nigeria.

Pastor Isah Jesse Abraham (crouching, second from right) and church members seal the grave of his son, Abdul'azzeez Joseph Isah, with concrete. His wife, Pastor Damaris Zainab Isah, is at far right.

Pastor Isah Jesse Abraham and his wife, Pastor Damaris
Zainab Isah, with members of their church after the grave
of Abdul'azzeez Joseph Isah was completed in a cemetery at
Taraba State, Nigeria.

The wreckage of the Covenant Salvation Bible Church building in Jalingo Taraba State, Nigeria. The church building was destroyed after Abdul'azzeez Joseph Isah, the ten-year-old son of the pastors of the church, was killed.

Pastor Isah Jesse Abraham and his wife, Pastor Damaris
Zainab Isah, inspect a parcel of land at Port-Harcourt Rivers
State, Nigeria, that was donated for the site of a new church.
The pastors moved to Port-Harcourt Rivers State in 2001
after their son was killed and their first church was destroyed.

Chapter Six

I Am Born Again

D ay and night, I gave myself to knowing the truth. During those days I saw God leading and guiding me on the right path to follow. After three weeks of reading and studying the Bible and the Quran, I saw the truth standing out about the Lordship of Jesus Christ.

All my life I recited Surah al-Fatihah 1:1–7 of the Quran as I mentioned in chapter one — until my conversion to Christianity. It says:

> In the name of Allah, the Beneficent, the Merciful. Praise be to Allah, Lord of the worlds, The Beneficent, the Merciful. Master of the day of judgment, Thee (alone) we worship; Thee (alone) we ask for help. Show us the straight path. The path of those whom Thou hast favored;

not (the path) of those who earn thine anger nor of those who go astray.

God, in His mercy, brought me through His truth to the path of those whom He has favored. He showed me the right path, and then gave me the grace to walk in it.

'Go and Tell Your Pastor'

"Go and tell your pastor I will come to church. If he will convince me that Jesus is the Son of God, I will give my life to Him and become a Christian."

That was the message I sent through my wife to the pastor of the church she was attending at the time of her conversion. That message was ringing in my heart even as I read in the Bible about the Sonship and Lordship of Jesus Christ. How can God Almighty in His Sovereignty, Divinity, Glory, and Majesty have a son? Seeing He does not have a wife, how can He beget a son? Though I was convicted, yet I was confused with this one question: How can God have a son? Because as a Muslim, from childhood, I was taught to believe that calling Jesus the Son of God is blasphemy against God, a sin of equalizing God with man. Only humans can have sons. Only humans are born and give birth themselves.

We Arrive at the Church

On a Sunday morning in November 1995, I followed my wife to the church to ask her pastor, how can God have a son? I read in the Bible that Jesus Christ is the only begotten son of God.

John 3:16

For God so loved the world that he gave His only begotten Son, that whosoever believes in Him should not perish but have everlasting life.

Quran 19:19 says that Jesus Christ is a faultless son, and one that is drawn near to Allah. And I also read in 1st John 5:4–5,

For whatever is born of God overcomes the world. And this is the victory that has overcome the world — our faith. Who is he who overcomes the world, but he who believes that Jesus is the Son of God?

I read the truth and I knew the truth that I had read, but my head was clouded by the spirit of Islamic religion that I was born into, and I found it difficult to accept the truth.

Quran 10:94

And if thou (Muhammad) art in doubt concerning that which We reveal unto thee, then question those who read the Scripture (that was) before thee. Verily the Truth from thy Lord hath come unto thee. So be not thou of the waverers.

I parked at the church and I told my wife, "Go inside. I will wait in the car, and when the service is over, then I will ask the pastor my question." I wrote the question on a piece of paper and put in my pocket.

But she said, "No, you can come inside the church and sit down."

And I said to her, "But I am a Muslim. How can I go into a church and sit among the Christians?"

She said again, "You can come in and sit down. It won't be a problem."

I went into the church with her and sat down. The pastor preached his sermon that Sunday morning on citizenship, saying that Christians are sons and daughters of God. Then, I remembered a verse in the Quran which says:

Quran 5:18a

The Jews and Christians say: We are sons of Allah and His loved ones...

Just as the Bible says in John 1:12:

But as many as received Him, to them gave He the right to become children of God, to those who believe in His name.

Romans 8:14
For as many as are led by the Spirit of God, these are sons of God.

The pastor continued his sermon saying that Christians are citizens of Heaven and are here on the earth as ambassadors of the Kingdom of Heaven, where Jesus Christ is the King who rules over it, and He is the Lord of Lords. While the pastor was preaching, I got all the answers to my questions that I intended to ask him afterward.

As he finished his preaching, he made an altar call for those who wanted to give their life to Jesus Christ by accepting Him in their hearts as Lord and personal Savior. He went on to say that no man can get to the Father except through Jesus Christ. I came to understand that God can see without eyes, can hear without physical ears, and can speak without using His tongue, so He (God) can have a Son without having a wife. This is the truth that makes God who He is. For with Him nothing is impossible. He can do anything. He can be anything at anytime and anywhere.

I Give My Life to Jesus Christ

At that moment, when the man of God was making that altar call, I felt the pressing urge of the Holy Spirit of God to step out and confess Jesus Christ as my Lord and Savior. Before the pastor could finish speaking, I was there standing in front of him.

When the pastor saw me standing before him, he shouted "Thank you, Jesus! Thank you, Jesus! Thank you, Jesus!" He shouted that over and over.

Then he led me to the Lord Jesus Christ. At that very moment I made my confession of faith and became a believer in Christ and established a serious relationship with the Lord Jesus. I became a child of God here on earth.

2nd Corinthians 5:20

Now then, we are ambassadors for Christ, as though God were pleading through us: we implore you on Christ's behalf, be reconciled to God.

Christianity Is Not a Religion, but a Relationship With God

Quran 21:73

And We made them chiefs who guide by Our command, and We inspired in them the doing of good deeds and the right establishment of worship and the giving of alms, and they were worshippers of Us (alone).

Please consider this for a while. Ask yourself, who are these 'Us' that are worthy of worship? And worshippers? The verse above says, "worshippers of Us." The Father, the Son, and the Holy Spirit are worshipped, and They received and accepted the worship of their worshippers.

Christianity is not a religion. It is a relationship between man and Almighty God. Relationship and religion are parallel. They are never the same. So many people today mistake relationship with God to be a religion, and they do not build a viable relationship with God.

Religion is man-made philosophy that will make you believe in the origin and nature of a man-made ideology. Islam is a call to believe in Muhammad's philosophy and ideology. On the other hand, Christianity is a call to a relationship with the Almighty God, the Creator of heaven and the earth, a relationship that culminates in worshipping the only true and living God in the person of Jesus Christ.

What Is Religion?

Religion is a system of faith and worship, the belief in and worship of a supernatural controlling power, especially a personal god or gods, which becomes a committed way of life to the people that accept such ideology.

What Is Relationship?

Relationship is a way in which two or more people behave and are involved with each other. It is the condition of being related, connected, or associated. Thus, Christianity is a way of life designed by God for us to follow and to create a good and a visible relationship with Him.

If Jesus can save me who was not converted into Islam but was born in it and grew up in it, was deeper into it, and had become a Ladan (one who calls for prayers) and later an Imam (one who lead prayers) in the mosque, then Jesus can save and use anybody, including you who are reading this book right now.

John 4:22–24

You worship what you do not know; we know what we worship, for salvation is of the Jews. But the hour is coming, and now is, when the true worshippers will worship the Father in spirit and truth; for the Father is seeking such to worship Him. God is Spirit, and those who worship Him must worship in spirit and truth.

You see, as I studied these verses in the Bible and the Quran, truth was revealed to me. Falsehood vanished away because falsehood is ever bound to vanish. Only the truth can stand the test of time. For where there is light, darkness can never stand, no matter its thickness, for light shines in the darkness and the darkness comprehend it not, and forever light will overcome darkness.

John 8:32

"And you shall know the truth, and the truth shall make you free."

I was made free by the truth of the Word of God. I am no longer in bondage of religiosity. I am free now to enjoy the life of the Son of God, who died and rose to give me life in abundance. Jesus is the only way to God, the truth that stands as the way of salvation, and the grace of God that brought unto us salvation (Titus 2:11).

John 14:6

Jesus said to him, "I am the way, the truth, and the life. No one comes to the Father except through me."

Quran 14:19

Hast thou not seen that Allah hath created the heavens and the earth with truth?

Jesus is that truth with which God created the heavens and the earth. It is as the apostle John put it, "God created the heaven with His Word, and the Word is the truth mentioned above. And with this truth the heavens and the earth were created. The truth is the Word, and the Word is the truth in the person of Jesus Christ."

Quran 11:7

And He it is Who created the heavens and the earth in the six Days — and His throne was upon the water ...

Genesis 1:31

Then God saw everything that He had made, and indeed it was very good. So the evening and the morning were the sixth day.

Genesis 2:1

Thus the heavens and the earth, and all the host of them, were finished.

Incredible truth! All these scriptures are what Jesus was sent by God to confirm to all of mankind in the Torah, which is the whole of the Old Testament. And Jesus Christ confirms it in the New Testament of the Word of God. Muslims call this the Injil: The Gospel of Jesus. Receiving the truth opens me to the salvation of God in my life. The Quran itself revealed that the Torah and the Gospel are to be confirmed.

Quran 3:2, 3, 4

Allah! There is no God save Him, the Alive, the Eternal. He hath revealed unto thee (Muhammad) the Scripture with truth, confirming that which was (revealed) before it, even as He revealed the Torah and the Gospel. Aforetime, for a

*guidance to mankind; and hath revealed
the criterion (of right and wrong) ...*

The Torah, which is the Old Testament, and the Gospel, which is the New Testament, are given by God aforetime for guidance to all mankind, and therein are the standards by which we all shall live, and by which we will know right and wrong. The potency of the word of God is contained in the Holy Scriptures given to us by Jesus Christ. Why do people of other religions not want to believe in this truth? I personally do not understand. For one to see the truth and not believe in it is pathetic.

Chapter Seven

The Divinity and the Humanity of Jesus Christ

T he authenticity of our Christian faith depends upon knowing and understanding the divinity and humanity of Jesus Christ. When Jesus was on earth, He lived a dual life. He was fully God and fully man. In His humanity, He was the son of man, and in His divinity, He was the son of God.

The Divinity of Jesus Christ

Quran 3:49

And will make him a messenger unto the Children of Israel, (saying): Lo! I come unto you with a sign from your Lord. Lo! I fashion for you out of clay the likeness of a bird, and I breathe into it and it is a bird, by Allah's leave. I heal him who was born blind, and the leper, and I raise the dead, by Allah's leave. And I announce unto you what ye eat and what ye store up in your houses. Lo! Herein verily is a portent for you, if ye are to be believers.

In Jesus' divinity, He walked upon the face of the earth as God among us. He healed those who were sick, opened the eyes of the blind, opened the ears of the deaf, opened the mouths of those who were dumb, and brought back to life those who were dead. In John 11:25, Jesus spoke of His divinity here on the earth as He proclaimed, "I am the resurrection and the Life."

Daniel 7:13-14

"I was watching in the night visions, And behold, One like the Son of Man, Coming with the clouds of heaven! He came to the Ancient of Days, and they brought Him near before Him. Then to Him was given dominion and glory and a kingdom, That all peoples, nations, and languages should serve Him. His dominion is an everlasting dominion, which shall not pass away, and His kingdom the one which shall not be destroyed."

These verses refer to Jesus Christ as the son of man who came to the Ancient of days as the Son of God approaching God the Father. We saw here, evidently, Jesus took the title "Son of Man," which was His favorite way of referring to Himself in the Gospels. He was given dominion, glory, and a kingdom that all peoples, nations, and languages should serve Him as King of kings and Lord of lords. The kingdom He received from His heavenly Father is a kingdom that cannot pass away or be destroyed. He received dominion that is an everlasting dominion. He reigns over this kingdom with power, might, and authority. Glory Hallelujah!

The divinity of Jesus is also revealed in Matthew 3:16–17:

> *When He had been baptized, Jesus came up immediately from the water; and behold, the heavens were opened to Him, and He saw the Spirit of God descending like a dove and alighting upon Him. And suddenly a voice came from heaven, saying, "This is My beloved Son, in whom I am well pleased."*

You also find the expression of the divinity of Christ in Matthew 17:5.

"While he was still speaking, behold, a bright cloud overshadowed them; and suddenly a voice came out of the cloud, saying, "This is My beloved Son, in whom I am well pleased. Hear Him!"

Jesus Christ Himself declared that He and the Father are one. In John 17:11 and John 17:22, Jesus said,

Now I am no more in the world, but these are in the world, and I come to You. Holy Father, keep through Your name those whom You have given Me, that they may be one as We are. ... And the glory which You gave Me I have given them, that they may be one just as We are one.

God and His Word are one, just as you and your word are one. Thus, we see the divinity of Jesus is established. Denying His divinity is refusing the truth of what the scriptures say about Him.

The Humanity of Jesus Christ

In various verses of the Bible, Jesus called Himself the Son of Man. He was vividly revealing to us His humanity as the God-man.

Matthew 12:40

For as Jonah was three days and three nights in the belly of the great fish, so will the Son of Man be three days and three nights in the heart of the earth.

John 3:14

And as Moses lifted up the serpent in the wilderness, even so must the Son of Man be lifted up...

In the verses of the scriptures above, Jesus revealed His humanity as the Son of Man. "He will be lifted up" symbolizes His crucifixion and being in the heart of the earth for three days and three nights symbolizes His death, burial, and resurrection. To get more understanding on these, let us look at some verses of the Bible and the Quran.

Isaiah 7:14

Therefore the Lord Himself will give you a sign: Behold the virgin shall conceive and bear a Son, and shall call His name Immanuel.

The name Immanuel means simply "God with us."

Isaiah 7:15

Curds and honey He shall eat, that He may know to refuse the evil and choose the good.

Isaiah 9:6–7

For unto us a Child is born, unto us a Son is given; and the government shall be upon His shoulder. And His name will be called Wonderful, Counselor, Mighty God, Everlasting Father, Prince of Peace. Of the increase of His government and peace there will be no end, upon the throne of David and over His kingdom, to order it and to establish it with judgment and justice from that time forward, even forever. The zeal of the Lord of hosts will perform this.

Only Jesus Christ came into the world with the attributes that qualify Him to live a life of divinity and humanity at the same time. In His humanity, He ate, slept, and walked upon the face of the earth as any normal human being does, yet He is God.

Matthew 1:23

"Behold, the virgin shall be with child, and bear a Son, and they shall call His

*name Immanuel," which is translated,
"God with us."*

Jesus Christ in His humanity here on earth was God with us.

John 1:14

And the Word became flesh and dwelt among us, and we beheld His glory, the glory as of the only begotten of the Father, full of grace and truth.

Matthew 9:6

"But that you may know that the Son of Man has power on earth to forgive sins" — then He said to the paralytic, "Arise, take up your bed, and go to your house."

Jesus Christ, in His humanity, has the power to forgive sins here on earth as the God-man. In His humanity, Jesus did anything a human being could do, except one: He did not sin. The God nature in Him kept Jesus away from sin in His humanity. In His humanity, Jesus was arrested, beaten by the Roman soldiers, spat upon, crucified, and pierced with a spear. On His head He wore the crown of thorns for the sins of mankind as He demonstrated His quality of benevolence.

The Quran says Jesus Christ was a faultless son from God who came as a sign and was illustrious in the world — Quran 3:49, 45; Quran 19:19.

Chapter Eight

Birth, Crucifixion, Death, Burial, Resurrection, and Ascension of Jesus

The last event in the earthly life of Jesus was His ascension into heaven. The ascension of the Lord Jesus cannot be told without first considering His birth, crucifixion, death, burial, and resurrection. The Bible makes it clear that Jesus ascended into heaven and that He will come back again. Jesus was greater than all the messengers that came before Him in many ways. None of them was born as Jesus was. None of them was crucified and died like Him. No other prophet was buried the way He was. None of all those who came before Him rose from death and none ascended into heaven as Jesus Christ ascended. And none of the prophets, except Jesus, will ever come back into the world.

The life Jesus lived here on earth was a clear pointer to His uniqueness and peculiarity that made Him so different. All the attributes of the life of Jesus revealed the glory, majesty, dominion, and power of the only begotten Son of God. Those attributes cannot and will not be found in any other. Both the Bible and the Quran agree that Jesus is unique and peculiar from His conception to His ascension into heaven.

Let us look at these step by step. Between His conception and birth and His ascension are His crucifixion, death, burial, and resurrection. Each of the above events identify Jesus, and no other, as the true savior of mankind.

The Conception and Birth of Jesus Christ

The birth of the Lord Jesus Christ was unique. No human being was ever born without the involvement of a man. Only the Lord Jesus Christ. His conception and birth were purely the involvement of divinity at work. His conception was of the Holy Spirit. Before His conception there was a prophecy given by Isaiah the prophet that a virgin would conceive and give birth to a son. Isaiah wrote this prophecy 700 years before Jesus Christ was born.

Isaiah 7:14

Therefore, the Lord Himself will give you a sign: Behold, the virgin shall conceive and bear a Son, and shall call his name Immanuel.

The fulfillment of this same prophecy of Isaiah is found in the Quran 4:171 that Jesus Christ is a Word from Allah, which He conveyed unto Mary, and He (Jesus) is a Spirit from Allah.

Quran 3:45, 49

(And remember) when the angels said O Mary! Lo! Allah giveth thee glad tidings of a word from Him, whose name is the Messiah, Jesus, son of Mary, illustrious in the world and the Hereafter, and one of those brought near (unto Allah). ... I came unto you with a sign from your Lord. ...

Quran 19:20-22

She said: How can I have a son when no mortal hath touched me, neither have I been unchaste? He said: So (it will be). Thy Lord saith: It is easy for Me and (it will be) that We may make of him a revelation for mankind and a mercy from Us and it is a thing ordained. And she conceived him, and she withdrew with him to a far place.

Quran 19:27

Then she brought him to her own folk, carrying him. They said: O Mary! Thou hath come with an amazing thing.

The conception and birth of the Lord Jesus Christ was such an amazing thing that only those who believe can grasp the meaning of what was done for humanity in it. The birth of Jesus brought Glory to God in the Highest and peace and good-will unto humanity. No birth was spoken about like that of Jesus.

Luke 2: 6–14

So it was, that while they were there, the days were completed for her to be delivered. And she brought forth her firstborn Son, and wrapped Him in swaddling cloths, and laid Him in a manger, because there was no room for them in the inn. Now there were in the same country shepherds living out in the fields, keeping watch over their flock by night. And, behold, an angel of the Lord stood before them, and the glory of the

> *Lord shone round around them, and they were greatly afraid. Then the angel said to them, "Do not be afraid, for behold, I bring you good tidings of great joy which will be to all people. For there is born to you this day in the city of David a Savior, who is Christ the Lord. And this will be the sign to you: You will find a Babe wrapped in swaddling cloths, lying in a manger. And suddenly there was with the angel a multitude of the heavenly host praising God and saying: "Glory to God in the highest, and on earth peace, goodwill toward men!"*

The birth of Jesus Christ gave to us a Savior. Besides Him, no other savior was given to mankind. Any other claim that is contrary to what the angel and the heavenly host said is a falsehood from the pit of hell that has no basis to stand at all! The only begotten Son of God, in the person of Jesus Christ, stands to be our Savior and was given by Father God a name that is above every other name. At the mention of the name of Jesus every knee in heaven, on earth, and beneath the earth shall bow.

Philippians 2:9–11

Therefore God also has highly exalted Him and given Him the name which is above every name, that at the name of Jesus every knee should bow, of those in heaven, and of those on earth, and of those under the earth, and that every tongue should confess that Jesus Christ is Lord, to the glory of God the Father.

Thus, He was highly exalted by God, the Creator of the heavens and the earth, to save mankind from their sins.

The Crucifixion of Jesus Christ

Jesus Christ came as a Savior to save mankind from sin. He is the Grace of God that brought salvation to all of humanity.

Titus 2:11

For the grace of God that brings salvation has appeared to all men ...

Jesus came and took our sins and nailed all of it on the cross. On the cross He shared His blood for the cleansing of the sins of mankind. He became the sacrificial lamb of God, and He, as the sacrificial lamb, offered Himself once and for all to save, redeem, sanctify, unify, and justify us, and to bring reconciliation between man and God.

His crucifixion became so necessary as a Savior, redeemer, sanctifier, unifier, justifier, and reconciler of whosoever believed in Him. He turned sin into righteousness. The crucifixion made Jesus Christ, who knew no sin, to become sin for our sake that He might become our righteousness, as we become His followers.

The crucifixion is full of mysteries that cannot be explained by man. God's divine revelation of the crucifixion reveals as much of Himself as He chooses. Jesus came from God just for that purpose alone. Jesus Christ knew that was the reason why He came into the world. Pilate was on his judgment seat when they brought Jesus before him. Jesus, knowing the reason why He came, said: "... *For this cause was I born, and for this cause came I into the world ...*" (John 18:37).

Acts 2:22–24, 36

Men of Israel, hear these words: Jesus of Nazareth, a Man attested by God to you by miracles, wonders, and signs which God did through Him in your midst, as you yourselves also know — Him, being delivered by the determined purpose and foreknowledge of God, you have taken by lawless hands, have crucified, and put to death; whom God raised up, having loosed the pains of death, because it was not possible that He should be held by it. ... Therefore let all the house of Israel know assuredly that God has made this Jesus, whom you crucified, both Lord and Christ.

Galatians 3:1

O foolish Galatians! Who has bewitched you that you should not obey the truth, before whose eyes Jesus Christ was clearly portrayed among you as crucified?

These are scriptural facts that made me realize the truth about the Crucifixion of Jesus. The cross was a means of His ascension into heaven. Without the crucifixion, no one would have talked about His ascension at all.

The crucifixion is mentioned in the Quran as the means of His ascension into heaven!

Quran 3:55

(And remember) when Allah said: O Jesus! Lo! I am gathering thee and

causing thee to ascend unto Me, and am cleansing thee of those who disbelieve and am setting those who follow thee above those who disbelieve until the Day of Resurrection. Then unto Me ye will (all) return, and I shall judge between you as to that wherein ye used to differ.

This verse states that the ascension of Jesus Christ was a thing predetermined by Allah. Most Muslims believe that Jesus ascended into heaven and returned to Allah without being crucified, but Jesus Himself referred to His crucifixion in the Quran.

Quran 19:33–34

Peace on me the day I was born, and the day I die, and the day I shall be raised alive. Such was Jesus, son of Mary: (this is) a statement of the truth concerning which they doubt.

Why and how in the world should anybody deny and disbelieve the crucifixion of Jesus when Jesus Himself talked about the day that He was to die on the cross? Here are the verses that present the denial:

Quran 4:157

And for their saying: We slew the messiah,
Jesus, son of Mary, Allah's messenger —
and they slew him not nor crucified him,
but it appeared so unto them; and lo!
Those who disagree concerning it are in
doubt thereof; they have no knowledge
thereof save pursuit of a conjecture; they
slew him not for certain.

This is the assertion of the Muslims, that it was made to look like Jesus was crucified, but He was not, and someone else took His place. But how and why in the world are people made to believe in this assertion and falsehood? Can God the Creator of Heaven and earth and all that is therein stoop so low to deceive His creation? Far be it from God to deceive those whom He created. It is demeaning for the Creator to deceive the people He created by Himself and for Himself! Does God have to deceive people to save His Messenger?

If the Quran says it was made to look like Jesus was crucified, but that someone else took His place and was crucified, then why would Allah violate the words of Jesus which say, "Peace shall be upon Him the day He was born, and the day He will die, and the day He will be raised alive?"

Of course, we all should know that one verse should be fulfilled before the next verse is fulfilled if what was said is truly the word of God! But see what the next verse says:

Quran 4:158

But Allah took him up unto Himself. Allah was ever Mighty, Wise.

Muslims claim Jesus was taken up to Heaven without Him dying and without Him rising from the dead. But what happens to the prophecy of Jesus, who said, "The day I die?" Have a rethink and believe in the truth. Jesus Christ, the son of the Living God, was the one that was crucified on that old rugged cross, not anyone else!

Matthew 27:32

Now as they came out, they found a man of Cyrene, Simon by name. Him they compelled to bear His cross.

Could this verse be the reason that Muslims claim that someone else was crucified in the place of Jesus Christ? The Holy Bible has brought out the truth!

Matthew 27:33–35

And when they had come out to a place called Golgotha, that is to say, Place of a Skull, they gave Him sour wine mingled with gall to drink. But when He had tasted it, He would not drink. Then they crucified Him, and divided His garments, casting lots, that it might be fulfilled which was spoken by the prophet: "They divided My garments among them, and for My clothing they cast lots."

Ephesians 2:16

... And that He might reconcile them both to God in one body through the cross, thereby putting to death the enmity.

It was on the cross that Christ reconciled us unto God and slayed the enmity that was between man and God.

Philippians 2:8

And being found in appearance as a man, He humbled Himself and became obedient to the point of death, even the death of the cross.

Colossians 1:20

... And by Him to reconcile all things to Himself, by Him, whether things on earth or things in heaven, having made peace through the blood of His cross.

It was the crucifixion of Jesus Christ on the cross that reconciled us with God, and it was the shedding of His blood on that cross that brought about the peace we enjoy in God today. The crucifixion of Jesus Christ has brought us innumerable benefits, so many that they cannot all be put on paper.

Colossians 2:13–14

And you, being dead in your trespasses and the uncircumcision of your flesh, He has made alive together with Him, having forgiven you all trespasses, having wiped out the handwriting of requirements that was against us, which was contrary to us. And He has taken it out of the way, having nailed it to the cross.

These and many more of the benefits of His crucifixion God arranged for us as we believe in the finished work of redemption by Jesus Christ on the cross!

The Death of Jesus Christ

Jesus died to set us free from the bondage of sin. He died on the cross that we may be alive unto God our maker. It was His death that qualified Him to be the mediator of the new covenant between God and man.

Romans 5:8

But God demonstrates His own love toward us, in that while we were still sinners, Christ died for us.

Galatians 6:10

Therefore, as we have opportunity, let us do good to all, especially to those who are of the household of faith.

Hebrews 9:15–17

And for this reason He is the Mediator of the new covenant, by means of death, for the redemption of the transgressions under the first covenant, that those who are called may receive the promise of eternal inheritance. For where there is a testament, there must also of necessity be the death of the testator. For a testament

is in force after men are dead, since it has
no power at all while the testator lives.

Quran 19:33
"... and the day I die ..."

Above are the words of Jesus Christ in that verse.

Quran 5:75
The messiah, son of Mary, was no other
than a messenger, messengers (the like
of whom) had passed away before him ...

The verse that follows explains the verses above.

Quran 3:144
Muhammad is but a messenger,
messengers (the like of whom) have
passed away before him ...

The second verse here explains the first one. Both verses are similarly worded. The first refers to Jesus Christ and the second refers to Muhammad. The Quran here is very clear to every truth-seeker.

The first verse made it clear that all prophets who came before Jesus Christ had died, and all Muslims accepted this to be true.

In the second verse, the same words are used to state or indicate that all prophets that came before Muhammad had died also. But the Bible reveals to us that Enoch did not die.

Genesis 5:24
> *And Enoch walked with God; and he was not, for God took him.*

Enoch went to heaven without dying.

Verses of the Quran above indicate that all prophets died. Enoch did not die, according to the Book of Hebrews.

Hebrews 11:5
> *By faith Enoch was taken away that he did not see death, "and was not found, because God had taken him"; for before he was taken he had this testimony, that he pleased God.*

Also, Elijah was taken up into heaven by God without him dying.

2nd Kings 2:11
> *Then it happened, as they continued on and talked, that suddenly a chariot of fire appeared with horses of fire, and*

> *separated the two of them; and Elijah
> went up by a whirlwind into heaven.*

These two prophets of God did not experience death but were translated into heaven. They were before Mohammad.

Since there is no other prophet between Jesus and Muhammad, the second verse could only have been revealed specifically to show that Jesus had died! The phrase "passed away," when it refers to a human being, refers to their death.

Quran 4:159

> *There is not one of the People of the
> Scripture [Christians] but will believe in
> him before his death ...*

Quran 3:55

> *(And remember) when Allah said: O
> Jesus! Lo! I am gathering thee and
> causing thee to ascend unto me, and am
> cleansing thee of those who disbelieve
> and am setting those who follow thee
> above those who disbelieve until the Day
> of Resurrection. Then unto Me ye will
> (all) return, and I shall judge between
> you as to that wherein ye used to differ.*

The above verse also proves that Jesus Christ died for exultation to God's presence. If Jesus Christ did not die, the verses of the Quran above would not make any sense at all!

The death of Jesus Christ on the cross was not like the death of mortal men. He died to set us free and to justify us that we might become partakers of the promises of God. That is why His death became a blessing — not a blessing for Him, but for all mankind. In His humanity, He took our place and died on that old, rugged cross to redeem us from the curses of the law being made a curse for us.

Galatians 3:13–14

Christ has redeemed us from the curse of the law, having become a curse for us (for it is written, "Cursed is everyone who hangs on a tree"), that the blessing of Abraham might come upon the Gentiles in Christ Jesus, that we might receive the promise of the Spirit through faith.

These are some of the numerous things that the death of Jesus Christ brought to us. No death of any prophet brought to humanity what the death of the Lord Jesus Christ brought. All the prophets who came had died before the coming of Jesus "except Enoch and Elijah who were translated into heaven" and their death did not bring any profit to mankind.

Quran 3:144

Muhammad is but a messenger, messengers (the like of whom) have passed away before him. Will it be that, when he dieth or is slain, ye will turn back on your heels? ...

On the morning that the prophet Muhammad died, Abu-Bakr, one of the prophet's disciples, came and found the people distracted. Omar, another of the prophet's disciples, told the people that it was a sin to say that the prophet was dead. Abu-Bakr ascertained the truth that Muhammad was dead, came back to the people, and cried, "Lo! As for him who worship Muhammad, Muhammad is dead, but as for him who worship Allah, Allah is alive and dieth not." Then, he recited the verse above to them, and it was as if the people had not known till that time that such a verse had been revealed.

In the Quran, the death of the prophet Muhammad was predicted. He died and he is still dead, and his death did nothing for mankind. But the death of Jesus brought salvation, restitution, redemption, sanctification, justification, and great deliverance from the shackles of sin.

Romans 6:1–11

What shall we say then? Shall we continue in sin that grace may abound? Certainly not! How shall we who died to sin live any longer in it? Or do you not know that as many of us as were baptized into Christ Jesus were baptized into His death? Therefore we were buried with Him through baptism into death, that just as Christ was raised from the dead by the glory of the Father, even so we also should walk in newness of life. For if we have been united together in the likeness of His death, certainly we also shall be in the likeness of His resurrection, knowing this, that our old man was crucified with Him, that the body of sin might be done away with, that we should no longer be slaves of sin. For he who has died has been freed from sin. Now if we died with Christ, we believe that we shall also live with Him, knowing that Christ, having been raised from the dead, dies no more. Death no longer has dominion over Him. For the death that He died, He died to sin

*once for all; but the life that He lives, He
lives to God. Likewise you also, reckon
yourselves to be dead indeed to sin, but
alive to God in Christ Jesus our Lord.*

These things that the death of the Lord did for mankind are beyond any human comprehension. They are enormous, magnanimous, marvelous, and awesome indeed. He stands different as King of all Kings, Lord of all Lords, Conqueror, Master of the Universe, Redeemer, and Savior of mankind!

The Burial of Jesus Christ

The burial of Jesus Christ refers to the burial of the body of Jesus, after His crucifixion, by a man named Joseph of Arimathea. In Jesus' humanity, He was arrested, judged by Pontius Pilate, crucified, died on the cross, and was buried. But death could not hold Him captive, because, even in the grave, Jesus Christ is Lord!

As I read through the Bible, I came to realize that it was Jesus, not an impostor, who was buried and right there in the grave He fought the battle that brought a triumphant victory to those who believed or will believe in Him.

Mark 15:43–47

Joseph of Arimathea, a prominent council member, who was himself waiting for the Kingdom of God, coming and taking courage, went in to Pilate and asked for the body of Jesus. Pilate marveled that He was already dead; and summoning the centurion, he asked him if He had been dead for some time. So when he found out from the centurion, he granted the body to Joseph. Then he bought fine linen, took Him down, and wrapped Him in the linen. And he laid Him in a tomb which had been hewn out of the rock, and rolled a stone against the door of the tomb.

The burial of the Lord Jesus was so significant that even where He was laid was of eternal value that God had to put it in His word! We all have sinned and come short of the Glory of God and deserve God's judgment.

Romans 3:23

… For all have sinned and fall short of the glory of God …

But God the father sent His only begotten Son to satisfy that judgment for those who believe in Him.

John 3:16

For God so loved the world that He gave his only begotten Son, that whoever believes in Him should not perish but have everlasting life.

Jesus Christ, the Creator of all things, the eternal Son of God, loved us so much that He died for our sins, taking the punishments that we all deserved, was buried, and rose from the dead for our justification, according to the Holy Bible, the eternal word of God.

If you truly believe and trust this in your heart, recognizing Jesus alone as your Savior, declaring Jesus as the Lord of your life, and standing on your declaration, you will be saved from judgment and spend eternity with God in Heaven.

That was what I did over twenty-two years ago and created a place for myself in eternity in Heaven. You too can do the same today!

The Resurrection of Jesus Christ

Jesus Christ was and is the only Prophet of God who died and rose from the dead triumphantly after His crucifixion, death, and burial, as a sign to mankind that He is above all and He stands to be the only Savior of mankind. The resurrection of

Jesus Christ is the hope of our salvation. Without the resurrection, the work of Salvation would have no meaning whatsoever.

Romans 10:8–10

But what does it say? "The word is near you, in your mouth and in your heart" (that is, the word of faith which we preach): that if you confess with your mouth the Lord Jesus and believe in your heart that God has raised Him from the dead, you will be saved. For with the heart one believes unto righteousness, and with the mouth confession is made unto salvation.

The resurrection of Jesus Christ from the dead over 2,000 years ago is still today mind-blowing to the kingdom of darkness. Nothing authenticates the work of redemption in the salvation of man but the resurrection of Jesus Christ. He was arrested, judged, crucified, died on the cross, and buried in his humanity, but rose from the dead triumphantly in His divinity. Divinity cannot be arrested, judged, crucified, die, and be buried in the grave. That was possible in the life of Jesus when He came into the world and took the form of man.

John 1:14

And the Word became flesh and dwelt among us, and we beheld His glory, the glory as of the only begotten of the Father, full of grace and truth.

Sin and death came and reigned in the world through the first Adam. Righteousness and resurrection into a newness of life came in the person of Jesus Christ, who is the last Adam. Understanding this will make any unbeliever believe the saving knowledge of the Lord Jesus Christ, without compromise. Both the Holy Bible and the Quran revealed to me the authenticity and truthfulness of the resurrection of Jesus Christ, and it was this truth that brought me into the saving knowledge of Jesus.

I believed it in my heart, and I was convicted to confess Jesus as my Lord and Savior. And this same truth remains potent to work in the life of whosoever comes to know Jesus Christ with an open heart. The Lord Jesus Christ Himself proclaimed that He is the resurrection and the life.

John 11:25

Jesus said to her, "I am the resurrection and the life. He who believes in Me, though he may die, he shall live."

On the day of Jesus' resurrection, He rose from the dead in His resurrected body to demonstrate what He proclaimed at the grave of Lazarus that He is the resurrection and the life! This is in fact demonstrated by the fact that only He, Jesus, was able to perform as the resurrection and the life that He claimed to be!

Quran 3:55

(And remember) when Allah said: O Jesus! Lo! I am gathering thee and causing thee to ascend unto Me, and am cleansing thee of those who disbelieve and am setting those who follow thee above those who disbelieve until the Day of Resurrection. Then unto me ye will (all) return, and I shall judge between you as to that wherein you used to differ.

The verse of the Quran above plainly portrays the death, resurrection, and ascension of Jesus Christ. Without resurrection there can never be the ascension. Jesus ascended into heaven because He was resurrected from the dead. The resurrection of Christ is the keystone of the Christian faith. It is the historical event upon which Christian doctrine stands. The great apostle Paul makes this very clear in his first letter to the church in Corinth.

1st Corinthians 15:12–25

Now if Christ is preached that He has been raised from the dead, how do some among you say that there is no resurrection of the dead? But if there is no resurrection of the dead, then Christ is not risen. And if Christ is not risen, then our preaching is empty and your faith is also empty. Yes, and we are found false witnesses of God, because we have testified of God that He raised up Christ, whom He did not raise up — if in fact the dead do not rise. For if the dead do not rise, then Christ is not risen. And if Christ is not risen, your faith is futile; you are still in your sins! Then also those who have fallen asleep in Christ have perished. If in this life only we have hope in Christ, we are of all men the most pitiable. But now Christ is risen from the dead, and has become the first fruits of those who have fallen asleep. For since by man came death, by Man also came the resurrection of the dead. For as in Adam all die, even so in Christ all shall be made alive. But each one in his own order: Christ the first fruits, afterward those who are Christ's at His coming.

> *Then comes the end, when He delivers
> the kingdom to God the Father, when He
> puts an end to all rule and all authority
> and power. For He must reign till He has
> put all enemies under His feet.*

His resurrection from the dead brought to him Glory, majesty, dominion, and the power to deliver to the Father the Kingdom, and to rule over the same Kingdom with authority and power. The resurrection of Christ is what demonstrated the importance and the frequency with which Jesus Christ is proclaimed to the world, right from the days of the apostles until today.

Philippians 3:10

> *That I may know Him and the power
> of His resurrection, and the fellowship
> of His sufferings, being conformed to
> His death.*

The Ascension of Jesus Christ

Luke 24:45–53

> *And He opened their understanding, that
> they might comprehend the Scriptures.
> Then He said to them, "Thus it is written,
> and thus it was necessary for the Christ to*

suffer and to rise from the dead the third day, and that repentance and remission of sins should be preached in His name to all nations, beginning at Jerusalem. And you are witnesses of these things. Behold, I send the Promise of My Father upon you; but tarry in the city of Jerusalem until you are endued with power from on high." And He led them out as far as to Bethany, and He lifted up His hands and blessed them. Now it came to pass, as He blessed them, that He was parted from them and carried up into heaven. And they worshipped Him, and returned to Jerusalem with great joy, and were continually in the temple praising and blessing God. Amen.

Jesus Christ is the very Word of God and the Spirit of God who left Heaven, His place of glory, and came into the world through the virgin birth. He proclaimed the message of the Kingdom of God with authority and power, healing and delivering all that was oppressed of the devil during His earthly ministry. He is the only begotten son of the Father and He was approved by miracles, wonders, and signs, and is full of grace and truth. He is the faultless Son of God. God raised Him to be above all creatures that were ever created by God, and He is the very Word with which all things were created, both in Heaven and on the earth.

Colossians 1:13–22

He has delivered us from the power of darkness and conveyed us into the kingdom of the Son of His love, in whom we have redemption through His blood, the forgiveness of sins. He is the image of the invisible God, the firstborn over all creation. For by Him all things were created that are in heaven and that are on the earth, visible and invisible, whether thrones or dominions or principalities or powers. All things were created through Him and for Him. And He is before all things, and in Him all things consist. And He is the head of the body, the church, who is the beginning, the firstborn from the dead, that in all things He may have the preeminence. For it pleased the Father that in Him all the fullness should dwell, and by Him to reconcile all things to Himself, whether things on earth or things in heaven, having made peace through the blood of His cross. And you, who once were alienated and

*enemies in your mind by wicked works,
yet now He has reconciled in the body of
His flesh through death, to present you
holy, and blameless, and above reproach
in His sight ...*

The above are some of the numerous benefits that the resurrection and ascension of Jesus Christ brought to us as believers in Christ. Anyone who aligns himself or herself with it will at once, automatically, become a beneficiary of it. The ascension of Jesus Christ brought unto us tremendous blessings that are unprecedented and beyond human comprehension. When Jesus rose from the dead, before His ascension into heaven, He blessed the disciples.

Luke 24:50
*And He led them out as far as Bethany, and
He lifted up His hands and blessed them.*

All the way from the birth of Jesus to the ascension of Christ into Heaven was a blessing to humanity. At his birth, the angel said to the shepherds that he brought to them good tidings of great joy. And that is a great blessing!

Luke 2:8–11

Now there were in the same country shepherds living out in the fields, keeping watch over their flock by night. And, behold, an angel of the Lord stood before them, and the glory of the Lord shone round around them, and they were greatly afraid. Then the angel said to them, "Do not be afraid, for behold, I bring you good tidings of great joy which will be to all people. For there is born to you this day in the city of David a Savior, who is Christ the Lord."

Before His ascension into heaven, this was what Jesus did:

Luke 24:45–53

And He opened their understanding, that they might comprehend the Scriptures. Then He said to them, "Thus it is written, and thus it was necessary for the Christ to suffer and to rise from the dead the third day, and that repentance and remission of sins should be preached in His name to all nations, beginning at Jerusalem. And you are witnesses of these things. Behold, I send the Promise of My Father upon

> *you; but tarry in the city of Jerusalem*
> *until you are endued with power from on*
> *high." And He led them out as far as to*
> *Bethany, and He lifted up His hands and*
> *blessed them. Now it came to pass while*
> *He blessed them, that He was parted*
> *from them and carried up into heaven.*
> *And they worshipped Him, and returned*
> *to Jerusalem with great joy, and were*
> *continually in the temple praising and*
> *blessing God. Amen.*

The resurrection of Christ came with tremendous blessings that brought great Joy that caused the disciples to worship, praise, and bless the name of the Lord. The resurrection is what brought the coming of the Holy Spirit upon them.

Acts 1:8

> *"But you shall receive power when the*
> *Holy Spirit has come upon you; and you*
> *shall be witnesses to Me in Jerusalem,*
> *and in all Judea and Samaria, and to the*
> *end of the earth."*

The Holy Spirit coming upon the believers serves as a seal of the blessing He released upon them, from the blessing after His resurrection to the blessing of His ascension. Jesus made humanity to take their right standing with God, as a means of completing the work of salvation He brought to mankind. The ascension of Christ was a blessing to us, and it was a means of exaltation for Jesus to the place of power and authority on high.

There is no way the ascension of Jesus Christ into heaven can be denied. Even the Quran did not deny the ascension of Jesus into heaven. But the Quran's version is that Jesus escaped death because God took Him up to Himself when the Jews came to kill Him, which means the Muslims denied the death and resurrection of Jesus Christ, but believed in His ascension into heaven.

Muslims also believe that Jesus is coming back. They believe the world will not end until Jesus comes back to undo the wrong belief about Him as the son of God. As long as Jesus is still up there in heaven, the world will not end.

What an interesting and smart way of avoiding truth: telling the half-truth! I am of the opinion that the denial of the truth about Christ's crucifixion, death, burial, and resurrection is due to ignorance of the word of God and of the life of Christ.

Quran 3:55

... I am gathering thee and causing thee to ascend unto me ...

This phrase confirmed to us that the Muslims also believed in the ascension of Jesus Christ. We also see "gathering thee," which can only refer to a corpse. This also is a proof of the death of Christ in the Quran, even though not preached by their clerics. And between the "gathering thee" and "causing thee to ascend" lay the resurrection.

Quran 4:157

... but it appeared so unto them ...

Allah said He (Jesus) will be gathered unto him, which can only happen after death, but they said it was not Him that died but that it only appeared so to them. This means Allah made them believe in something that never happened. But Allah said Jesus would die.

Quran 4:159

There is not one of the People of the Scripture but will believe in him before his death ...

The verse above says, "Before his death," which means He will die, yet they said He did not die. Tell me, what do we believe? Jesus Himself said He would die and ascend. Muslims say that He did not.

Quran 19:33

Peace on me the day I was born, and the day I die, and the day I shall be raised alive!

These three days spoken of by Jesus Himself have proven every man to be a liar, and God alone be true.

Quran 4:158

But Allah took him up unto Himself.

The following scriptures in the Bible were the verses that abolished the wrong assertions that were inculcated in me when I was a Muslim. These scriptures convinced me to believe in the crucifixion, death, burial, and resurrection of Jesus. David said in Psalm 68:18:

You have ascended on high, You have led captivity captive; You have received gifts among men, even from the rebellious, that the Lord God might dwell there.

John 6:62

What then if you should see the Son of Man ascend where He was before?

John 3:13

No one has ascended to heaven, but He who came down from heaven, that is, the Son of Man who is in heaven.

The apostle Mark said in Mark 16:19:

So then, after the Lord had spoken to them, He was received up into heaven, and sat down at the right hand of God.

The devil is a liar! You better believe the truth before it is too late! The apostle Luke said in Acts 1:1–3, 9–11:

The former account I made, O Theophilus, of all that Jesus began both to do and teach, until the day in which He was taken up, after He through the Holy Spirit had given commandments to the apostles whom He had chosen, to whom He also presented Himself alive after His suffering by many infallible proofs, being seen by them during forty days and speaking of the things pertaining to the kingdom of God. ... Now when He had spoken these things, while they watched, He was taken up, and a cloud received Him out of their sight. And while they looked steadfastly toward heaven as He went up, behold, two men stood by them in white apparel, who also said, "Men of Galilee, why do you stand gazing up into heaven? This same Jesus, who was taken up from you into heaven, will so come in like manner as you saw Him go into heaven."

Ephesians 4:8–10

Therefore He says: "When He ascended on high, He led captivity captive, and gave gifts to men" (Now this, "He ascended" — what does it mean but that He also first descended into the lower parts of the earth? He who descended is also the One who ascended far above all the heavens, that He might fill all things).

I pray in the name of Jesus Christ of Nazareth for everyone reading this book right now that you too will come to the saving knowledge of the Lord Jesus, and to also respond to that same knowledge by accepting Jesus Christ as your Lord and Savior! For the same Jesus who saved me is rich unto all that will call upon Him for salvation today, and he or she shall be saved! There is no miracle that will ever happen to you greater than the miracle of salvation provided in the Lord Jesus Christ!

Chapter Nine

The Persecution Begins

After I gave my life to the Lord Jesus Christ on November 12, 1995, and openly declared my salvation, my family members learned that I had become a Christian and had started attending church. That was when the intense persecution started.

A week after my conversion, I received a message from my childhood friend, Adamu Audu, that I was needed at the mosque where I had been the Imam. But a friend warned that there was a plot to kill me if I appeared at the mosque. This was because my childhood friend Adamu Audu had told those at the mosque and at my family house that I had become a Christian and had started going to church with my wife and child. He too was a member of the mosque and his parents lived next to my family house. We happened to be neighbors in the compound where I rented an apartment when I moved out of my family house and married my wife in 1993.

Adamu Audu was already renting and living there with his wife. He had told me about the apartment to lease. Because Adamu's home was close to mine and I had to pass his home when going out or coming in, he was the first to notice that I was going to church with my wife. He never confronted me, but he went to tell them at the mosque and at my family house, where my uncle who I grew up with lived with his family. Upon hearing that I was needed at the mosque — to be killed — I refused to go.

In January 1996, my father sent my younger brother Kabiru to tell me that my father wanted to see me at the family house. But I refused to go because I knew the danger that awaited me there, because my family house and the mosque where I was an Imam were just five minutes walking distance, and I knew that I could not go to my family house without someone in the community knowing. I refused to go.

My Father Comes to Me

After my father saw that I had refused, he came to my house three days later, in the evening. He said, "Isah, I want you to come with me right now to the family house. Your uncle Alhaji Adamu, your sister's husband Usman, and your aunty Hajiya Uwarbarai are at the family house waiting for me."

I knew there was danger if I dared to follow him, so I said to him, "Alhaji, just go I will be right behind you." But I never went.

On seeing that I did not go, my family decided to get my attention by sending my younger brother Kabiru to my house. He normally spent weekends at our house. My son Abdul'azzeez and my wife were fond of him. He came, as usual, two days after my father's visit.

When my son saw him, he was excited and said, "Uncle what did you bring for me?"

Kabiru asked him, "What do you want?"

He said, "A biscuit," what Americans call a cookie.

So Kabiru took him out to get him a biscuit and left my wife at home. But ten minutes moved to an hour, and they were not back. My wife was worried, because the store where they were to buy the biscuit was just a two-minute walk away.

I came back from my job at the bank at about 8 p.m. and my wife told me that my brother Kabiru had come to the house at 5:30 p.m. and took Abdul'azzeez to get him a biscuit at the store. They still had not returned. On hearing that, I knew something was wrong and it dawned on me that they wanted to get me by kidnapping my son. I knew who had taken him. I also knew their intentions. But it was night, so I decided to leave it until morning.

In the morning, I decided to go to my job and ask for some days off work to look for my son. When I reached my workplace at 7 a.m., a friend was waiting for me at the gate.

My friend said that my son was taken by my younger brother Kabiru and that he had traveled with him to Kura in Kano State, and that it was a plan to trap me. He said that all the family members were summoned to be at our family house in Kura Kano State, and that everyone was to gather at sunset because they knew I would have to close my workplace before I came for my son.

On hearing the whereabouts of my son, I went into the office and took the day off work. I drove straight to Kura, a three-and-half hour journey.

At My Family House in Kura Kano State

On reaching there I met a lot of family members at the family house with my father, but most of them happened to be women, so I went to my dad and asked, "Where is my son?"

He said, "Isah, is it true that you are now an infidel?"

I did not reply to his question. I said, "Whatever you want to hear, I will tell you, but not now."

Then my son heard my voice, and he ran out from my mother's room towards me. I picked him up and ran to my car and took off. That was how God helped me to escape death that day. It was easy for me because most of the people I met in the house were women and there are restrictions in Islam on how women should relate with or approach a man, even if he is her brother, once the women become adults, especially if they are married. There was nothing they could do.

At My Apartment on Zongo Road Kaduna

I arrived at my apartment on Zongo Road Kaduna safely with my son, but I knew that I had to do something very fast or I and my family, that is my wife and my son, would soon be history. While I was trying to figure out what to do, after our arrival home from Kura in January 1996, I, my wife, and my son went for Bible study at the Household of Love Church Unguwan Yelwa Sabon Tasha Kaduna. This was on a Wednesday, and we came back home at about 10 p.m. and found our dog Snoopy had been killed. Our neighbors said that a group of men came asking after us. They carried machetes, swords, sticks, and knives. When they tried entering our apartment, our dog would not let them in, so they beat him to death.

On hearing that, I was afraid of what would happen to us. But it was already late. I thought of going to report the attack at the police, but I remembered that if I did that it would be at the police station in my community, and that the officers were Muslims, so I might not get justice. Besides, Muslims believe that dogs are forbidden animals and that the Prophet Muhammad never entered a house that had a dog. The police were not likely to see killing a dog as a crime. I decided that I would leave the area with my family in the morning.

My intention was to leave as early as 5 a.m. In fact, we could not sleep because my wife and son were terrified by the incident. And around 4:30 a.m. I heard noise in the front of my apartment.

A group of men were shouting, "Isah, come out! We have come to make you an example to anyone who would rebel against Islam. We have come today to fulfill the mandate of Allah through his prophet Mohammed." And they were hitting my front door, which was a glass door with an iron frame. They broke the glass, but the iron held fast.

My wife and son were crying, and I told my wife not to cry. I said to her, "Take care of our son. I will go and open the door and I believe God will take absolute control, for I know we serve a living God who will not allow them to carry out their evil intentions on us."

I opened the door and I saw about fifteen men with weapons of different kinds, machetes, knives, swords, sticks, and iron rods, just as we had been told by our neighbors.

I said, "Jesus help me and save us." I stood quietly looking at them as they came into my sitting room.

One of them said, "Let's finish them."

Another said, "No! Let's beat the madness out of them."

Then another said, "No! Let us just kill them. After all, that is what they deserve. That is their reward for denying the faith."

I was standing there, watching, and praying inside of me for God to save me and my family. After twenty minutes or so they could not agree on what they should do with us. Before I knew it, right before me, they started arguing among themselves while I stood and watched without saying a word.

Suddenly, they dragged me and pushed me out. They asked my wife and son to get out of the apartment, and then they started throwing our belongings out. They destroyed our property, locked the door of the apartment, and left with the key. We were left outside with nowhere to go on that cold January morning in 1995.

I later learned from a friend that my land-lord sent those men to kill us because he could not stand to see an infidel, especially one who had been a Muslim but had denied the Islamic faith, living in his house. He told them to kill me, my wife, and my son. He believed he would do Allah a favor by killing us, and that Allah would give him and the men that carried out the assignment a reward. How we escaped death that day only God knows.

Another Apartment

Some hours after they left, I succeeded in calming my wife and son. They were really trau-matized with what happened. We packed some of our belongings that had not been destroyed and we went looking for a new apartment for my wife and son and what was left of our belongings.

I found a two-bedroom apartment, went to the bank, withdrew money, and paid the landlord. I got my wife and son, who had been outside in the cold from around 6 a.m. to 5 p.m., and took them to the new apartment. I thought to myself, "Thank

God that finally my family and I have a place to enter, take a shower, eat, and rest."

But I guess I underestimated the gravity of my offense to the Muslim community. Little did I know that the story of my conversion to Christianity had spread widely around my community, and that all the Muslims in the area were warned not to associate with me or have anything to do with me. Every Muslim was told that anyone seen associating with me would partake of the same punishment that was due to me: death.

As I got to the new apartment with my wife and son, the new landlord was standing at the entrance to the apartment. I greeted him but he did not answer.

The first thing that came out of his mouth was, "You infidel, a cursed person, a denier of Allah and his prophet! You want to rub your sin curse on me? I can never rent my house to an infidel! You and your money are cursed."

He threw the money I had paid him for the apartment back at me. I picked up the money and turned, not knowing where to go. I left our property outside. I loaded my wife and my son into our car, and I drove for an hour to the highway.

I sat thinking about all that had happened, and I asked myself, "Isah, when and how did you get to this point?" None of my family members wanted to have anything to do with me. All my friends that I had grown up with had rejected me.

Tears ran down my face. Then I said to myself, "Now I have to be strong for my wife and for my son." This was around 9 p.m. I resolved that if my family members, relatives, and friends had rejected me, I would go to the church and ask to pass the night in the church hall with my wife and son. In the morning I would look for another apartment.

We Get a Place to Stay

On reaching the church I met the security man and told him all my problems and challenges and my intention for coming to the church. While I was still telling the security man my story, the resident pastor of the church, the Rev. Tony Owulale, came out of the church office on his way home. When he saw me, my wife, and my son at that hour of the night, he asked what was wrong. I narrated the whole issue to him, and he was moved by my story. Because that was the church we were attending, he already knew our story of conversion.

He offered to give us a room in his home until we could get a place of our own. We were so happy. We went that night to stay in his house at Narayi in Kaduna South. That was a Friday and the next day was Saturday, so I did not have to report to work at the bank. The next morning, I hired a truck and moved our remaining belongings to the pastor's house through the help of some youths in the church.

I Lose My Job Because of My Newfound Faith

On Monday, January 8, 1996, I went to my office at about 8 a.m. to work as usual. I noticed that some of my co-workers were staring at me. I did not know why, and I felt it was strange. At about 10 a.m. I was told by the manager's secretary that my attention was needed at the manager's office. Upon entering the office, I was presented a white envelope and was told to leave. I was surprised, but I did not ask any questions.

I walked back to my desk and sat down. I opened the envelope and read that I was being suspended for six months without pay. Workers in Nigeria are paid a salary monthly. I expected to be paid my December 1995 salary in January of 1996. I had worked for it, but nothing was paid to me. I had worked as an account officer in the loan department for almost eight years. I had never had a quarrel or any warning letter. Why then was I suspended without pay? I had not committed any offense that I knew of. I went back to the manager and asked him why I had been suspended.

He replied, "Isah, it has come to our knowledge that you have committed Riddah. You have denied the faith of Islam. You have denied Allah and his prophet. But because you are a good worker, we believe something has gotten into your head. Therefore, we want to give you time to think about your stupid and crazy decision. Go and think about what you want, Allah or Jesus, but know that if you choose Jesus you lose your job and even your life. But if you come back to Islam, and you accept Allah and his prophet, you will get back your job, and a promotion."

But I chose Jesus. And the news got to my family house and the mosque where I served as an Imam before my conversion to Christianity. This was because my father's friend, Alhaji Yusuf, who had helped me get the job, was also a friend of the manager at my place of work, and he was aware of all that was happening. When I told the manager that I had chosen Jesus, the manager told Alhaji Yusuf, who took the news to my family house at Doka and the mosque.

A Twelve-Member Committee
Is Sent to Kill Me

That same week of January 12, 1996, as I was driving along Badikko Road Kaduna expressway, using my car as a taxi so that I could feed my wife and son, and pay my bills, a friend stopped me along the highway.

He said to me, "Isah, don't go further. There is an ambush by a committee of men to bring you dead or alive to the mosque because of what Alhaji Yusuf said in the mosque about your decision. They are set to kill you if they get you. Run for your life. The men had been asked to look for you everywhere in the city of Kaduna. If they see you, they will accomplish what they were told to do."

Then, he hurriedly left so that no one would see him talking to me. That was the last time I saw or heard from that friend, who had saved me from persecution four times.

Our Trip to Kopshu Village

On hearing that information, I took a turn and went back to the pastor's house. Early the next day, January 13, 1996, I took my wife and my son and travelled to Kopshu Village in Plateau State, a remote village where my wife's parents came from.

More than 99 percent of the people that live in Kopshu Village are Christian. The village had no telephone, tap water, hospital, electricity, or good access roads. That made it difficult for anyone to trace us there. We stayed there until the second week of April 1996. We returned to the pastor's house and I intended to complete a room in the unfinished three-room bungalow that I built at Rigasa Kaduna and to move my family there.

When we arrived, I dug a well and began preparing the house for my family to move into it. One afternoon in May 1996, I went to the house and found several men working in it. I confronted one of the men and asked what he was doing on my property. He said that my father had sold the house to him. I was devastated. What little money I had was spent fixing one room and digging the well. And my father sold the house without my consent. My father had given me the gift of that land when I told him I wanted to build my house, but I had built the house myself.

I Decide to Seek Justice

I felt very bad and remembered all that had happened and was still happening to me — how I was suspended from work for six months without pay, how the manager refused to pay me the month of

December salary that I had earned, how I had been thrown out of two apartments that I had rented, and how I was threatened with death. I remembered how my father had sold my house without my consent and then did not give me the money or anything out of it. I thought of the twelve-member committee that had been sent to take my life.

I decided in May 1996 to seek justice and see if the law could fight for me, if I could be protected from the committee that sought to kill me, and if I could have justice for what my landlord had done to me: evicting my family and sending men to kill me. They killed our dog, destroyed our property, and threw me out of a house for which I had paid three months in advance. In Nigeria, you pay rent annually and I still had three months left.

But the police officer in charge of that police station, on hearing that I had been a Muslim and had become a Christian, turned the case against me. To Muslims, the Quran is above the law of Nigeria. I went to a chief judge whom I had helped to secure loans from my place of work, and I asked him to help me. He was interested in the case. He asked for the information of those involved, which I told him. He asked me to go and come back to see him the next day. I thanked him and left. When I returned to his office the next day, to my greatest surprise, I met my landlord and two other men.

The chief judge said to me, "So this is what you have done, denying Allah and his prophet. In fact, you deserve to die. If I ever see you in my office again or hear that you went to any other court, I will personally put you in prison myself and I will make sure you are killed there, you infidel!"

On hearing this from the judge, I held my wife's hand, and we hurriedly left the premises immediately.

I had to hide myself. We could not go out in the daytime. We were still living with the pastor. I decided to leave Kaduna completely. I discussed leaving Kaduna with a member of the church we were attending. He gave me the address of his friend in Port Harcourt Rivers State. In June 1996, I sold my car and traveled to Port Harcourt. I remained in Port Harcourt and I attended Bible school at Faith Bible Institute, No. 1 Faith Avenue, Rumuomasi Port Harcourt.

Two times our church building was destroyed. First at Madganari Maiduguri Borno State. Muslims threw stones at us as we were preaching and teaching the truth of the Word of God. They brought down the church building completely in October 1999.

We came to Jalingo in Taraba State in December 20, 1999. Our first-born son was murdered on September 1, 2000, in Jalingo Taraba state. Our church building in Jalingo Taraba State was destroyed in April because of our newfound faith.

As a result of the threats against us for our conversion into Christianity, we moved about from place to place, hiding ourselves and our identities for over twenty-three years in search of a covering and security.

We came to Bwari, a district in Abuja, the capital of Nigeria, on April 12, 2004, where we continued the preaching of the Word of God, even with the persecution and with so many threats to our lives.

In July 2009, the Muslim group Boko Haram emerged, seeking to establish an Islamic State in Nigeria. Boko Haram and Fulani herdsmen kill Christians and burn churches. With Muslim persecution and murders of Christians, the threats against my family from my Muslim relatives and acquaintances became more and more serious. Any Muslims in Nigeria who knew about my family sought to kill us.

The last death threat we received was from an Islamic group that had come to Bwari in Abuja on December 25, 2017. I, my wife, and our children would have been killed if not for a woman who heard of the evil plot and sent us a message to move out of Bwari. That same Islamic group burned the entire market in Bwari Abuja on Christmas day in 2017.

To escape this persecution and threats to our lives, we came to the United States of America. We were waiting to be granted religious asylum by the government of this great nation of great love, great peace, and great justice, a nation that obeys and respects the rule of law. Here I and my wife and our five children found peace, love, and protection to live and to serve the Lord Jesus Christ without fear of persecution, death, or terror.

END

About the Author

The Rev. Isah Jesse Abraham is the founder of Covenant Salvation Ministries and was the Senior Pastor of Covenant Salvation Bible Church in Abuja Nigeria, where he co-pastored with his wife, Damaris Zainab Isah. Covenant Salvation is a charismatic congregation with a mandate to take salvation to the families of the world. Isaiah 49:5–6 and Acts 13:47 describe the ministry of this man of God.

Rev. Isah was born into a strong Muslim Hausa Fulani Family from Kano State in Nigeria. Rev. Isah was converted to Christianity in November 1995 and is now a vibrant preacher of the gospel of the Lord Jesus Christ. Many miracles have accompanied Rev. Isah's Gospel to Nations Power Crusade, and thousands have been saved into the Kingdom. He is also a sought-after speaker for churches, conferences, and seminars. He holds an annual Sense of Destiny Impact Conference with awesome testimonies recorded to the Glory of God.

Rev. Isah testifies to his conversion from Islam to Christianity through his knowledge of the Quran and the Bible, especially in:

- The Lordship of Jesus Christ identified in the Quran
- The person of the Holy Spirit identified in the Quran
- The divinity of Jesus Christ revealed in the Quran
- The death and resurrection of Jesus Christ as revealed in the Quran
- The sonship of the person of Jesus Christ identified in the Quran
- The identification of Jesus Christ as the sinless prophet in the Quran.

His testimony has been an eye opener to Christians and Muslims alike.

Rev. Isah Jesse Abraham can be described as a passionate lover of God's Word!

The Ministry

Covenant Salvation Ministries is the umbrella body of the entire vision as received from the Lord in the year 1998, which birthed:

- Covenant Salvation Bible Church, the church operational base of the ministries
- Gospel to Nations Power Crusade, the Crusade arm and the missionary-sending department of the ministry
- Isah's Home Library, the publishing arm of the ministry, reaching the world through books, magazines, tracts, etc.
- Covenant Salvation Bible Institute, the training arm of the ministry, which equips men and women through teaching that will propel them into achieving God's vision and purpose for their lives and into fulfilling their lives and destinies.

All the arms of Covenant Salvation Ministries work together as a force in one Spirit to achieve the vision and mandate given by God for the ministry — the sole purpose of the calling.

Aims and Objectives of the Ministry

- To take the life God (Covenant) to the lost and needy all over the world through the teaching and preaching of the undiluted word of God. Acts 1:8, Isaiah 49:5–6. and Acts 13:47 are the mandate scriptures of the commission (ministry).
- To create a strong winning network through crusades, radio, television, and the print media — Matthew 28:19–20.
- To create a strong intercessory group ready to storm against the enemy.
- To create Operation Help, to provide food, clothing, housing, medical care, and education for the less-privileged, widows, orphans, the poor, and the needy.

Our Faith and Beliefs

We believe in the Trinity: God the Father, God the Son, and God the Holy Spirit.

We believe that salvation is by faith through grace.

We believe that Jesus Christ died, was buried, and rose from the dead on the third day for our justification.

We believe that we are ambassadors of the Kingdom of God here on the earth.

We believe in the Lordship of Jesus Christ.

We believe that Satan is down, and Jesus Christ is exulted.

We believe we are seated together with Christ in dominion and authority.

We believe we shall reign with Jesus when He comes in His glory as we serve Him faithfully.

We believe we walk by faith and not by sight.

We believe we have the mind of Christ.

We believe we are redeemed from the curse of the law.

We believe we can do all things through Christ which strengthens us.

We believe the Kingdom of God is in power.

We believe and confess these to be true in Jesus Christ's name!

CPSIA information can be obtained
at www.ICGtesting.com
Printed in the USA
LVHW072322200821
695736LV00010B/281

9 781662 821837